Praise for SPIRITUALS
That Will Change Your Life

"Great spirituals are songs you listen to but in Henry Carrigan's book he shows that great spirituals should be read as well. We need to be reminded that these songs are the foundation of gospel music as well as rock'n'roll, country, rhythm and blues—indeed all of American music."
—Don Cusic, author, teacher, historian, songwriter, producer and executive

"Through strong faith, deep musical knowledge, a critic's eye, and a historian's understanding, Henry's affable masterclass through these religious classics offers pure joy and enlightenment. His insider's expertise in a wealth of musical traditions offers widely inclusive descriptions of how these songs have given strength to the Civil Rights Movement as well as Appalachian family singers. At a time when the world seems to be coming apart, we need this book as a reminder of how these deeply spiritual songs should unite us all."
—Aaron Cohen, author, *Aretha Franklin's Amazing Grace*

"Henry gracefully explores why these fifteen songs reach down deep and endure within us. A must-read for all!"
—Rebekah Long Speer, Bluegrass/Americana artist, wife of gospel singer Ben Speer

"Great songs stand the test of time and behind every song there is a story that we never get to hear, but thanks to author Henry L. Carrigan Jr. we will learn about these spirituals that will change your life. Read and learn and be blessed."
—Joseph S. Bonsall, 45-year member of The Oak Ridge Boys, and the author of ten books

"From my earliest memories, through the voice of my grandmother, spiritual songs became a thread that continues to connect me to something beyond this world. Written so blessedly, Carrigan hits upon many of the very songs that move me and he reminds me that words and melody will always be part of my soul."
—**Donna Ulisse**, singer/songwriter

"In this shallow, disorienting world of information overload, Henry brings forth a transformative tool: the soaring voices, lyrics and musical heart of spirituals. Through its insights into musical history as well as personal and theological reflections, *Fifteen Spirituals* invites us into a profound look at grace, hope, and faith. It is perfect for Bible study, spiritual direction or daily personal devotions."
—**Rev. Susan Sparks,** pastor, Madison Avenue Baptist Church;
author, *Laugh Your Way to Grace*

"I enjoyed reading this book, and not just reading, but listening to each of the fifteen spirituals recorded by different artists. My favorite parts of the book are the reflections of the songs that give us insight to how we can apply the messages from each song to our daily lives. This book will have an impact on your life."
—**Becky Perry Brown,** author of *Going Our Way: My Life with Jim Ed Brown*

"Henry Carrigan takes the deep dive into the heart of Gospel Music, reminding the reader that 'great music changes us and great gospel music changes how we live.' The soul of this book is alive and his scholarly devotion to the spirit of the music is pure joy, faith, and freedom."
—**Emily Duff,** singer/songwriter

"Music is in Henry Carrigan's blood, and his love for it bleeds onto the page. His writing is soulful, powerful, and—best of all—illuminating."
—**Christine Ohlman,** songwriter and vocalist, the *Saturday Night Live* band

Fifteen SPIRITUALS
That Will Change Your Life

HENRY L. CARRIGAN JR.

PARACLETE PRESS
Brewster, Massachusetts

Dedicated to
my mother, Suetta Tisdale Carrigan,
and to the memory of
my father, Henry Lowell Carrigan,
and to the memory of
my grandparents.

2019 First Printing

Fifteen Spirituals That Will Change Your Life
Copyright © 2019 by Henry L. Carrigan Jr.

ISBN 978-1-64060-086-7

Scripture quotations, unless otherwise noted, are from the Revised Standard
Version of the Bible (RSV). Copyright © 1946, 1952, and 1971 the Division of
Christian Education of the National Council of the Churches of Christ in the United
States of America. Used by permission. All rights reserved.

The Paraclete Press name and logo (dove on cross) are trademarks of Paraclete Press, Inc.

Library of Congress Cataloging-in-Publication Data
Names: Carrigan, Henry L., 1954- author.
Title: Fifteen spirituals that will change your life / Henry L. Carrigan, Jr.
Description: Brewster, MA : Paraclete Press, Inc., 2019.
Identifiers: LCCN 2019000744 | ISBN 9781640600867 (trade paper)
Subjects: LCSH: Spirituals (Songs)—History and criticism. | Gospel
music—History and criticism.
Classification: LCC ML3187 .C37 2019 | DDC 782.25/309—dc23
LC record available at https://lccn.loc.gov/2019000744

10 9 8 7 6 5 4 3 2 1

Published by Paraclete Press
Brewster, Massachusetts www.paracletepress.com
Printed in the United States of America

CONTENTS

INTRODUCTION

I N 1972, SOUL SINGER ARETHA FRANKLIN released a record that is her finest album. *Amazing Grace* sold over two million copies in the United States, and in 1973 she won the Grammy for Best Soul Gospel Performance. Recorded live in the New Temple Missionary Baptist Church in Los Angeles in January 1972, *Amazing Grace* showcases not only Franklin's gospel roots but also her command of vocal range and phrasing.

Franklin is a soul stirrer, exciting her audience and getting them on their feet, shouting with them, encouraging them to sing and shout and to give their souls to the Master, in "Give Yourself to Jesus." The moans of the blues carry into the aching tenderness of a song like "Give Yourself to Jesus," into which she slips the music of "God Will Take Care of You." Franklin demonstrates her brilliance when she blends the musical themes of two songs that have the same musical structure into the medley of "You've Got a Friend" and "Precious Lord, Take My Hand." Finally, her version of "Amazing Grace" features her own lyrical piano playing, as she opens the hymn with a moan that's backed by the choir; she then draws out the lines of the song's first verse in a sparse way as she plays call and response with the notes of the piano. As she moves into the second verse, there's a moment when the congregation begins to shout with acclamation and to shout in call and response to her vocals. If you can listen to only one Aretha Franklin song, this should be it: "Amazing Grace" on the 1972 *Amazing Grace* album illustrates every feature of Franklin's artistry. No other recording demonstrates the range of her voice, her ability to get inside of notes and stretch them to wrench every emotion out of listeners, her brilliant piano playing, and her devotion to the power of music to evoke love.

There's also no better introduction to the moving, transforming power of gospel music than Franklin's version of "Amazing Grace." Even if you didn't grow up going to church or participating in any kind of religious community, or listening to hymns or contemporary religious music, you can't help being moved by Franklin's astonishing vocals, her exquisite musical timing, her emotional investment in the lyrics, her passionate delivery of the music. For the moments she's singing, she is one with the music itself. The notes have become part of the fabric of her being, and with every breath she exhales music. This one performance can be transformative, lifting us out of ourselves so that we transcend, even momentarily, our everyday worries, fears, anxieties, and darkness. Aretha Franklin's performance of "Amazing Grace" can redeem us, can change us, can save us—change our hearts, save us from being mired in the miasmic quandaries of our daily lives, redeem us by turning our hearts and minds and souls to embrace the grace that enables us to love God and others and to repair broken relationships with others and our world with mercy and justice.

Franklin's performance may be the very best illustration that gospel music transcends divisions and boundaries, both musical and social. When we listen closely to her performance, it changes us. We can no longer listen to "Amazing Grace" the same way again, for once we've listened to Franklin's version, other versions lack the passionate engagement with the song's themes of hope, mercy, love, and joy (the final verse of the song radiates the joy of God's enduring love, and the enduring love we are to share with others). Once we've listened to Franklin's performance of the song, we can no longer promote division but seek instead to erase lines of hatred that make others less than human. Great music changes us. Great gospel music changes how we live.

Music touches people's hearts in deep and enduring ways that words often fail to do. When people hear a certain song, they recall powerfully the feelings they connect with certain events they associate with first hearing that song. Music helps people live through desperate situations, provides soothing comfort in times of loss, evokes sweet memories of certain relationships, connects individuals to one another in a kind of musical community (we're "one in the spirit" when we sing certain songs congregationally, but we're also part of one another when we hear a certain song that recalls a particular time and place in our lives), evokes powerful stirrings of hope, faith, and love, and carries us to places beyond ourselves where we connect with others and with God.

Spirituals and gospel songs are especially powerful evocations of faith, hope, and love. The very music itself, while often familiar to its hearers, transcends the anxieties and plodding uncertainties of daily life. These songs acknowledge the hopelessness and the despair of everyday life while at the same time lifting us out of ourselves to another plane. Spirituals are born out of the field shouts and hollers of slaves in the American South and are characterized by a repetitious call and refrain that offers the singers—for spirituals are songs that we should be singing and not just hearing—a way to identify with the pain of others, as well as a way to fly away above it. Spirituals and gospel music developed first in the black church and then evolved in white Southern churches in forms referred to as country gospel and bluegrass gospel, each of which has its own style. But no matter the particular gospel style, the music has despair, salvation, love, hope, and transcendence at its core.

Fifteen Spirituals That Will Change Your Life is a short guide to the transforming power of fifteen different gospel songs, many of which are so familiar to many of us that we no longer hear the force of the lyrics and we no longer feel moved by the power of the music. This book invites you to hear these songs again, as if for the first time, to listen carefully to both the music and the lyrics, for the rhythms and the ways that the notes of the songs weave under and around each other, giving the song its peculiar quality. There are thousands of versions, both instrumental and sung, of "Amazing Grace," but no version is the same as any other, even though the lyrics have not changed for centuries. It's the music itself that sets the tone, that draws us in, that catches our attention, that attracts us to listen more than once to the song or to sing it often. Once the music captures us, we sway to the rhythms, cry to the interplay of vocals and instruments, or rejoice to the warming of our hearts when the organ and vocals swell in unison. *Fifteen Spirituals That Will Change Your Life* listens closely to the songs and asks you to do so, too, to hear what you have never heard before in a familiar gospel song—and offers reflections on those themes.

The book's focus is broad, exploring not only traditional spirituals—such as "Steal Away to Jesus" and "Swing Low, Sweet Chariot"—but also gospel songs that have their origins in the blues—such as "Keep Your Lamps Trimmed and Burning"—and contemporary songs—such as "If Heaven Never Was Promised to Me"—whose roots reach to traditional spirituals. Although I recognize the differences between spirituals and gospel songs, I have most often used the phrase "gospel songs" to refer to the songs discussed here, acknowledging that gospel music grows out of its roots in the blues and traditional spirituals.

While every chapter offers a brief history of the song and its composition, *Fifteen Spirituals That Will Change Your Life* is not a history of spirituals or gospel music. There are very good books that offer these histories or significant portions of these histories—such as Bil Carpenter's *Uncloudy Days: The Gospel Music Encyclopedia*, Don Cusic's *Saved by Song: A History of Gospel and Christian Music*, Robert Darden's *People Get Ready! A New History of Gospel Music*, Anthony Heilbut's *The Gospel Sound*, and Bob Marovich's *A City Called Heaven: Chicago and the Birth of Gospel Music*, for example. I have provided a list of selected readings for any readers interested in the deep background of certain songs or authors.

Every chapter of *Fifteen Spirituals That Will Change Your Life* opens with some brief history and background on the song, and then moves on to a more detailed analysis of the music and gospel themes on which the chapter focuses. The analyses explore the musical structure and the lyrics of each song and often compare various versions in order to point out differences of expression that can offer different ways of hearing the song's meanings. The final section of each chapter offers a brief reflection on the song, its possible applications, questions you might ask yourself, and ways that it might inspire you.

The best way to read *Fifteen Spirituals That Will Change Your Life* is to listen to various versions of these songs as you read about them. Find a quiet place and pull out your albums, or CDs, or cassette tapes, or queue up these versions of the songs on a streaming service such as Spotify or Pandora, and let the music wash over you; float away with it, dance to it, sing with it, cry over it, and rejoice with it as you read the book and reflect on the transformative power of these *Fifteen Spirituals That Will Change Your Life*. I hope you do. And I hope they do.

ꝺNE
AMAZING GRACE

BACKGROUND

IN LATE 2018, THE GOSPEL HALL OF FAME and Country Music Hall of Fame quartet the Oak Ridge Boys performed "Amazing Grace" at the funeral of former president George H. W. Bush, who had requested that they perform it at the funeral. In 2016, President Barack Obama sang "Amazing Grace" at the memorial service for Clementa Pinckney, who died in a shooting at a black church in Charleston, South Carolina. Obama's act prompted folk singer Joan Baez, who had sung the song in the 1960s as a folk song, to write "When My President Sang Amazing Grace" and record it on her last studio album in 2017. More than three thousand recordings of the song exist, and the artists who have recorded "Amazing Grace" range from rock singer Rod Stewart, folk singer Judy Collins, gospel greats Sam Cooke and the Soul Stirrers, and country artists Johnny Cash, Alan Jackson, and Reba McEntire, among many others. "Amazing Grace" can also be sung to the theme from the television show *Gilligan's Island*.

The story of the song's origin is familiar and told very often. There have even been movie versions of the telling. In the mid-eighteenth century, John Newton wrote "Amazing Grace" as a result of a dramatic personal experience of conversion. While Newton wasn't a religious person before his experience, he eventually sought ordination as an Anglican priest. Like his father,

Newton lived a life at sea in the service of the Royal Navy; after his stint in the Navy, he became the captain of a slave ship. In 1748, his ship almost capsized in a violent storm off the coast of Ireland, and he almost drowned during the incident. During the storm, he cried to God for mercy, converting to Christianity. Although he continued to work in the slave trade for a few years following the near shipwreck, he gave it up in 1754 and worked with the well-known abolitionist William Wilberforce to end the trade.

Newton's interest in religion grew as a result of reading Thomas à Kempis's *Imitation of Christ* and as he listened to the preaching of George Whitfield and Charles Wesley. As his religious commitment developed, he studied for the ministry and was ordained. Once he was appointed as a clergyman, he started writing hymns, and in 1779 he wrote "Amazing Grace" to illustrate one of his sermons. The song's themes of mercy, redemption, and God's love and grace endure into our own times.

The slave trade was finally abolished, at least in Britain, when Parliament passed the Slave Trade Act of 1807. John Newton died at eighty-two, just before Christmas, later that same year.

"AMAZING GRACE"

ONE OF THE MOST POPULAR AND MOVING VERSIONS of "Amazing Grace" is by the Blind Boys of Alabama. The group sings the song to the tune of the traditional folk song, "The House of the Rising Sun." Sonically, the tunes are the same, so Newton's lyrics sung over the minor chord shouts of an old folk blues song dramatically illustrate the inextricable bonds of human yearnings for grace and human desire to overcome the misery of their shortcomings. The Blind Boys of Alabama's version highlights the rousing character of gospel music and the ways that it can touch deeply the troubled souls of humans, convicting them of their unworthiness before God while at the same time prompting them to gratitude for God's grace to them.

The opening two lines of "Amazing Grace" combine this duality—praising the honeyed sound of God's gracious love while admitting human shortcomings: "Amazing grace! How sweet the sound / That saved a wretch like me!" The second line, though, contains an archaic word that sounds strange to our ears. When do we refer to ourselves or others as wretches? What is a wretch? In our world we seldom, if ever, speak or write about the wretchedness of the human condition or the wretchedness of individuals. *Wretch* refers to someone who is either unhappy or unfortunate, or someone who is despicable or for whom we have contempt. Both senses of the word apply in the second line, for the writer thinks of himself as an unfortunate person who once almost lost his life in a shipwreck, but he's also despicable because he traded in human flesh, which he now realizes, after his conversion, separates him from God. The writer also feels wretched because of his separation from God, but because of God's grace he can now be reconciled to God and others. Thus, grace echoes with a "sweet sound" and is beyond comprehension and description—"amazing."

The last two lines of the opening verse of "Amazing Grace" may be the most famous in Christian music: "I once was lost, but now am found / Was blind, but now I see." The theme of blindness and sight floats through the entire song as a key to its meaning. The singer wanders for years not seeing the injustices he's committing toward others; he turns his eyes away and pretends he doesn't see others committing the same acts. His sight is clouded by the fogs of inequality, yet he has no one to help clear those fogs away from his vision. Ironically, it's through hearing the sound of grace that he now sees a vision of God's grace. Without sight, he's lost; with this new vision, he has found his right relationship with God.

The second verse of "Amazing Grace" intensifies the wandering uncertainty and wretchedness of the first verse, but the power of God's grace grows stronger relative to the wretchedness in the second verse. Notice, too, that in this verse the action of grace does not occur over a long period of time; God's grace lifts the shadows of sin, darkness, and fear immediately upon conversion: "the hour I first believed." The immediacy of God's grace teaches the singer about his wretchedness: "'Twas grace that taught my heart to fear." If the singer had not experienced God's grace, he would not have known his actions were wrong or not consistent with God's love for him and others. God's grace not only gives the singer a glimpse of his shortcomings, but also opens in him the fear of God's punishment for such mistreatment of others. Not only that, but God's grace teaches the singer to tremble at God's awesome love. God's love and grace relieve the singer's fears, though, and God's generosity and forgiveness are precious gifts to the singer. The sweet sound and precious character of God's grace constitute a force stronger than any human fears or human inadequacies.

The third verse of "Amazing Grace" illustrates that the process of reaching the one moment where grace first appears is a long one. The singer travels through territory filled with "dangers, toils, and snares," obstacles that stand between the grace of God and the singer. The beauty of this verse is that grace acts as a dynamic force that underlies all human activity; God's grace and redemption operate in our lives, even when we cannot see them or feel them working. On another level, this verse could also refer to the slaves who traveled across treacherous seas in the cargo holds of ships such as the one that John Newton captained. Before they faced the toils of slavery, they were captured in the snares of slave traders. They faced the dangers of not only the ocean passage but also the life of enslaved men and women on plantations in American colonies. Above all, the verse depicts an enslavement to forces beyond our control—whether physical or spiritual—but operating beneath these forces is God's grace that protects us and leads us to a new world of freedom and redemption. The last two lines of the verse focus on the dynamic character of God's grace: "Grace hath brought me safe thus far / And grace will lead me home." The liberating power of God's grace protects us on every journey we make through the darkness of forces that would cause us to doubt, cause us to grieve, cause us to mourn, cause us to sin against others by treating them as less than human, and cause us to be less than fully human.

The fourth verse of "Amazing Grace" celebrates the promise of a grace-filled life, once the singer chooses to accept God's gift of amazing grace. Moreover, God's grace and goodness endures through time, even to the close of the age, as Jesus teaches. The opening line of the verse affirms the goodness that comes with God's grace and God's promise: "The Lord has promised good to me." God has given the singer the means by which to recognize this grace—Jesus and the Bible—for "the Word secures my hope," according to the singer. God reveals God's self in limited ways to humans—through nature, through the Bible, and through Jesus. In all these ways, God reveals patterns of grace in our daily lives that we can follow as we seek to embrace and to follow God's goodness and mercy in our own actions. As the third line indicates, God will be our protector—"shield"—and enliven us with God's presence—"Portion"—as long as we live—"as long as life endures." "Amazing Grace" moves from the moments we recognize our shortcomings to the immediacy of God's grace as it operates in our lives to the ongoing goodness and mercy of God's grace in our daily lives.

The final verse of "Amazing Grace" illustrates both the enduring character of God's grace and our response to this unmerited gift. Because God loves us unconditionally with a grace and mercy we don't merit, God deserves our worship and praise while we are on this earth. In fact, singing this song, "Amazing Grace," is one way we offer our praises and thanks to the God who has been always been providing us with the vision to see the needs of those around us. Praising and worshiping God involves taking care of the world and others, and acting toward them with the same mercy and love with which God has acted toward us. The last verse of "Amazing Grace" focuses on final revelation and the everlasting nature of God's grace and our worship. In the first line, the singer imagines the world God has promised following this earthly life when we'll reign with God forever: "When we've been there ten thousand years." This multiplies tenfold the thousand-year reign of Christ described in Revelation 20 to glorify and exalt the perfection of God. In the second line, we who have received God's grace and who have joined God in this everlasting reign are dazzling creatures, like the angels. God's grace has transformed us and continues to transform us, even after we have become creatures in God's eternal kingdom. Even in this transformed state, when we see God face-to-face, we continue to praise God as we did when we first heard the sweet sound of amazing grace, found our sight, and began to share the beauty and wonder of God's grace with others.

REFLECTION

"Amazing Grace" is such a familiar gospel song that we sometimes sing it without hearing the lyrics fully. To receive grace requires an admission of our shortcomings. It requires that we admit we have often treated others and ourselves as less than God fully intended us to treat them. It requires that we admit that we have sinned and are in need of God's love, God's forgiveness, and God's redeeming power. Can we hear the words of "Amazing Grace" anew when we live in a world that often looks for easy answers and cheap grace, in a world that seldom acknowledges human shortcomings? How can we hear the words of this familiar song in a fresh way?

Choose several versions of "Amazing Grace" and listen to them. Try to find a version of the song that is completely unfamiliar to you. Listen carefully to these versions, and hear the ways they move you from the initial stages of grace to the final stages of grace. How does the musical structure of each song elevate the goodness of God's grace? How does the sonic structure of each song evoke the sweet sound of God's grace and evoke in us the yearning for God's love and mercy? Choose your favorite version, and listen to it at least twice a day, once in the morning before the busyness of your day begins, and once in the evening as you reflect on the events of the day. In what ways do you feel God's grace during your morning listening? In what ways do you find glimpses of God's grace in your evening listening? Where have you seen God's grace in your daily life? Where do you see patterns of grace in your daily life? How can you share God's grace with others as God has shared God's grace with you?

When we listen closely, we hear our entire lives in faith described in "Amazing Grace," from the "hour we first believed" and the moments we gained our "sight" and "found" our way to the recognition that God's grace has carried us through the dangers and fears that have lead us to this present moment and the affirmation of God's enduring love and mercy. When we listen to a version of "Amazing Grace" such as Aretha Franklin's elevated and stratospheric performance of the song in her 1972 live concert, we hear in the very music itself the ups and downs of life, the pains and joys through which we pass daily, and the exalted beauty and transformative amazement of God's grace. For these reasons, "Amazing Grace" is a gospel song that will change your life.

Two
PRECIOUS LORD,
TAKE MY HAND

LIKE MANY GOSPEL MUSICIANS, Thomas A. Dorsey started out playing the blues. The Georgia native, whose mother played the organ and whose father was a Baptist preacher, found his passion playing blues piano under the names Barrelhouse Tommy and Georgia Tom, even playing with blues greats such as Ma Rainey and Tampa Red. When he was nineteen he moved to Chicago, pursuing his music in various blues and jazz bands, eventually starting his own band.

Dorsey had a nervous breakdown a few years later and left music behind. During his recovery, a minister friend told him not to give up music entirely but to think about returning to the church to play the church music with which he had grown up. Although the path wasn't easy, since many in the church had a hard time accepting a secular musician as a church musician, Dorsey never gave up, and he eventually became the choir leader at Chicago's Pilgrim Baptist Church. He also founded the first independent publishing house for black Gospel music, the Dorsey House of Music. It is Thomas Dorsey, in fact, who came up with the term "gospel music" to describe his style of music and the style he led in churches, and so he is often referred to as the Father of Gospel Music.

The story of "Precious Lord, Take My Hand" is a familiar one. In August 1832, Dorsey was invited to go to St. Louis to sell some sheet music. His pregnant wife, Nettie, was expecting to give birth at any moment, and Dorsey wasn't comfortable leaving her in Chicago. But she encouraged him to go. Dorsey had been in St. Louis just a few days when he received a telegram saying that Nettie was having difficulty with her childbirth. When he called home, he discovered that she had died, and he hurried back to Chicago. As he struggled and grieved for his wife, he then learned that his son had also died during the night. A few weeks later the despondent Dorsey was playing an old melody, "Must Jesus Bear the Cross Alone," on the piano and started to write the words to the song that became "Precious Lord, Take My Hand." He introduced it a few weeks later at Ebenezer Baptist Church where the congregation responded right away to the song's emotional immediacy. On one of Dorsey's earliest recorded versions, he poignantly shares this story behind the song, telling his audience that after the death of Nettie and his son, he started to go back to the blues, but he stuck to gospel music. He says that his words came like drops of water from the crevice of a rock above and seemed to drop in line: "Precious Lord, take me home."

Martin Luther King Jr. called "Precious Lord, Take My Hand" his favorite song, and gospel great Mahalia Jackson sang it at his funeral, at his request. "Precious Lord, Take My Hand" has become one of America's most-beloved gospel songs.

"PRECIOUS LORD, TAKE MY HAND"

LIKE MANY OTHER GOSPEL SONGS, "Precious Lord, Take My Hand" grapples with loss and despair and grief. Many of the other songs covered in this book also plead for God's comfort, love, and guidance, and like many other songs, Dorsey's song envisions God in an anthropomorphic fashion, with hands that can reach out and hold Dorsey's own hands during his overwhelming grief. "Precious Lord, Take My Hand" pleads for an intimate touch during a time when the singer feels as if everyone in the world has left him alone to deal with his misery and sorrow.

Every version of this gospel song moves at a measured and almost stately pace, allowing the singers to reach far down into themselves to embrace their mourning, their sadness, their sorrow, their desperation, their weakness, and to lay those feelings before God, asking God to lift them out of the darkness and to hold them in God's loving embrace. Thomas Dorsey's own version includes his emotional retelling of the story of the events that led him to write the song. Mahalia Jackson opens her song drawing out every phrase of every line of the opening verse—which is also the song's refrain—over the strains of an organ and the spare chords and rolls of a piano. Sister Rosetta Tharpe propels her shuffling version with her biting lead guitar notes that play call and response with the swelling chords of a Hammond B3 organ. Aretha Franklin draws out each note of the song's opening line— and she does the same with each line of the song—weaving her own rolling piano chords beneath her words. When Franklin sings the song, she captures the longing, the pain, and the exquisite need for God's presence in her life.

"Precious Lord, Take My Hand" opens with a plea for God to come and to stand by the side of the singer, who is so stricken with grief that he can barely stand. (On the night he returned home, Dorsey was so overcome with grief that he fainted as he got out of his car.) The opening line—"Precious Lord, take my hand"—is repeated as a prayer and refrain at the end of each verse, where its order is inverted to "Take my hand, precious Lord" (and the song is often seen with the title "Take My Hand, Precious Lord") to emphasize the singer's need for God's presence. The opening verse states the themes of the song, circling back to those themes in other verses of the song.

The singer asks God to take him by the hand to "lead me on, let me stand," for the singer is "tired, weak, and worn." The singer states his mental and physical condition in a clear and emphatic fashion with the phrase "I am": "I am tired, I am weak, I am worn." What's more, the conditions that have brought on these states of being are darkness—of loss, of fear, of death—and storminess—being tossed by the waves of doubt and isolation and loneliness. In the middle of this dark night of the soul and body, the singer craves closeness and illumination. "Come close to me, God," the singer pleads; "bring light to my darkness so I can find my way home," he pleads. The singer asks God to accompany him on a journey from this darkness into the light, showing him the path: "Lead me on . . . Through the storm, through the night / Lead me on to the light / Take my hand, precious Lord, lead me home." This gospel song is just one of many that pray for God and God's light to lead: "Lead Me, Guide Me," "Lead On, O Cloud Presence," "Lead, Kindly Light," and "Lead Me, Lord" are examples.

The second verse of "Precious Lord, Take My Hand" intensifies the singer's plea and reiterates the bleak condition in which he finds himself. The first line of the verse asks God to stay by the singer's side—"to linger near"—as his "way grows drear." The singer pleads for God not only to remain near him, but also to listen when he cries out for God's help in a dark moment: "When my light is almost gone / Hear my cry, hear my call." The images in these lines can easily apply to a dying person; as the person lingers on the edge between life and death, she asks her God to linger near, to be by her side, so that God can accompany her, lead her, to an eternal home ("precious Lord, lead me home.") In addition, at the edge of death, one's light is almost gone, and those who are dying often pray that God hears their call to take them home. In the penultimate line of this verse, the singer asks God to "take my hand lest I fall." If we think of the song referring, on one level, to death, then the singer prays here for God to lift him up in God's arms so that God can carry the singer on his final journey. If the song reflects the condition of the singer following loss and sorrow, then the line pleads for strength to stand strong through this dark time. The final line of the second verse is the song's refrain, which reiterates the desire for God to hold the singer's hand to lead him out of the darkness to the light of a new day and the comfort and love of home.

The third verse opens yet again on the darkness in which the singer finds himself. The lines in this verse offer the best illustrations of images that would contribute to a reading of the "Precious Lord, Take My Hand" as the plea of a dying person, praying for God to hold her hand and guide her on this journey to a new home. "When the darkness appears and the night draws near / And the day is past and gone / At the river I stand," the singer proclaims; she prays to God to "guide my feet, hold my hand." The key image in this verse—"at the river I stand"—illustrates the abyss that separates the earthly world from the eternal, heavenly realm. In biblical stories, rivers separate the old and tired world of weariness and oppression and the new world of life and freedom. God always accompanies God's people as they stand at the edge of the river, and these people pray for the support of their God in crossing the river to this new land. In Christian traditions, these stories of crossing rivers become images of moving from an earthly kingdom to eternal worlds. On another level, this verse intensifies the singer's darkness that surrounds him as the heaviness of his loss and sorrow and grief grows more insufferable. In the darkness of this situation, when all light is gone, the singer stands on the edge between hope and despair. Giving up hope leads to drowning in despair, but with God's guidance the singer can move away from the edge of despair to the brilliant light of hope. The last line of the verse, as in the other verses, prays fervently for God to take the singer's hand and lead him home.

"Precious Lord, Take Me Home" allows us to embrace the darkness in our lives that may be debilitating and from which we feel we may never recover, and out of which we feel we may never come into the light.

REFLECTION

All of us shuffle through the darkness that falls when a loved one dies, when we lose a job, when we struggle with addictions, when a once-vital relationship falters and crumbles apart, when we experience doubts about our faith, or when we struggle desperately to meet the needs of our families. "Precious Lord, Take My Hand" reminds us that light shines in the middle of our darkness, and we can petition God to lead us toward that light and a place where we can flourish.

Where are you experiencing darkness in your life today? What events in your life have led to you feeling your light is almost gone? When do you feel tired, weak, and worn? When do you feel too weak to stand? When have you felt that your life is falling apart so swiftly that you no longer can see the path ahead of you? When have you lost hope as you journey through your dark night? When and where do you feel the storm winds of life blowing harshly across your paths? How have you tried to reach the light? Where do you see glimpses of light in the middle of your darkness? How can singing or listening to "Precious Lord, Take My Hand" give you hope and lead you into the light from your darkness?

Listen to several versions of "Precious Lord, Take My Hand." Listen carefully to the differences in the musical structure of each version. Which version moves you the most? Which version captures the joyous praise floating through the song? Which version captures the darkness of your world? Which version gives you the most comfort in your darkness? Can you hear the sorrow in Thomas Dorsey's version? The celebration in Sister Rosetta Tharpe's version? The enduring sorrow of Aretha Franklin's version? Which version offers the most meaningful images of hope and comfort?

"Precious Lord, Take My Hand" illustrates the ways in which blues and jazz weave their way into gospel songs. Whether it's a piano-based version or a guitar-driven rendition, this gospel song incorporates the moaning and shouting of the blues, providing the sonic foundation from which the song can ascend to the heights of sonic spiritual acclamation. The combination of sorrow mingled with hope, expressed in a moving blues-gospel style, is the reason that "Precious Lord, Take My Hand" is a gospel song that will change your life.

*T*HREE
WADE IN THE WATER

———•——————

BACKGROUND

EXILE AND EXODUS, escape and freedom, stealing away and flying away are enduring themes of spirituals and gospel songs. Many spirituals grew directly out of the excruciating pain and unbounded desire to break the chains of a dehumanizing system of slavery that shackled and chained the bodies and spirits of millions of black men, women, and children in the American South from the late eighteenth century until the mid-twentieth century. While the physical bonds of slavery might have ended for some—and of course those bonds were supposed to be broken for all enslaved people—with the Emancipation Proclamation of 1863, and the subsequent end of the American Civil War in 1865, the mental, social, and spiritual shackles on black people continued to bind them to a less-than-human location in society. Slavery may have ended, but it was followed by Jim Crow and all manner of discriminatory practices based on white racial prejudice. In many ways, those bonds still encircle individuals even into the twenty-first century.

The Civil Rights Movement of the mid-1960s adopted many spirituals—such as "Wade in the Water," "Steal Away to Jesus," "Swing Low, Sweet Chariot"—as songs of protest, comfort, and hope. The Staple Singers delivered what's probably the most famous modern version of "Wade in the Water," for example, in

1965 during the Civil Rights Movement, and the song became an anthem for the burgeoning protest movement. In the early twenty-first century, "Wade in the Water" reminds us that, even when we're suffering in exile, God provides a way beyond our present troubles, often showing us signs by which we can escape them, even if the paths by which God leads us may be rough and rocky. We embark on our journey to freedom, led by God through the roiling waters stirred up by injustice and oppression, with the promise that redemption from oppression and suffering lies just on the banks on the other side of the waters.

As with many spirituals, the origins and authorship of "Wade in the Water" are lost in the shadows of history. Although the song is sometimes attributed to the American abolitionist and political activist Harriet Tubman, who reportedly used the lyrics of this spiritual to direct slaves to stations along the Underground Railroad, there is no clear evidence that she wrote the song. Some of the song's lyrics, especially the refrain ("wade in the water, children"), could have been directions to slaves fleeing captivity to stay off the roads and walk in the water to throw off the men and dogs tracking them.

"Wade in the Water" had been circulating orally—sung by individuals and by groups—in the latter part of the nineteenth century, but the spiritual was not published until 1901 when John Wesley Work Jr., who directed the Fisk Jubilee Singers, and his brother, Frederick Jerome Work, included it in their song collection *New Jubilee Songs as Sung by the Fisk Jubilee Singers.* Much like Alan Lomax—who later would collect field songs and blues songs from various regions across the world—the Work brothers

THREE ⟍ WADE IN THE WATER 25

collected slave songs and spirituals and published them, and John Work also led his Jubilee Singers in singing these songs. Even though the Fisk Jubilee Singers included "Wade in the Water"—as well as other spirituals and slave songs—in their performances, the Sunset Four made the first commercial recording of the spiritual in Chicago in 1925. Since then, many artists have recorded the song, including a lively, syncopated jazz instrumental by the Ramsey Lewis Trio, an airy and spacious trumpet-driven instrumental by Herb Alpert and the Tijuana Brass, and a hypnotic, slow boiling version by pianist Billy Preston.

"WADE IN THE WATER"

"Wade in the Water" recounts a journey—a momentous journey from bondage to freedom. The pilgrimage involves crossing boundaries, moving across swirling waters to cross over from lands where loss and pain reign to lands where hope and healing reign. Those crossing the rivers find themselves now embracing a new freedom of self and society in which they can control their own futures in ways they've never been able to do before. The song takes biblical stories of enslaved peoples crossing bodies of water to freedom and a new life as its basis, shaping those earlier stories to clothe the experiences of other enslaved peoples searching to cross over into freedom in a new land. The song's refrain—"Wade in the water / Wade in the water, children / Wade in the water / God's a-going to trouble the water"—counsels those gathered to make the journey to step into the roiling waters that both disguise their tracks from those searching for them as they make their escape and lead them across a boundary to freedom. This refrain may have provided covert directions to slaves, as many spirituals did, to step into water—the Ohio River, in this case—to hide their tracks as they made their way to freedom along the circuitous paths of the Underground Railroad.

The final line of the refrain—"God's a-going to trouble the water"—might sound quite strange to us today. After all, when does God trouble waters? What does it mean to "trouble the water"? Why would God do that? As with many spirituals, "Wade in the Water" draws many of its images from the Bible and bases its message on biblical allusions. In this case, the song draws a phrase directly from the Gospel of John 5:7: "The sick man answered him, 'Sir, I have no man to put me into the pool when the water is troubled.'" In the story in John, Jesus walks up to a pool of water in Jerusalem that is purported to have healing powers; several disabled individuals—who, according to the story, cannot walk because of paralysis in their legs or other injuries to their legs—have made the trip there to wade into the pool's healing waters. Jesus observes one man, who had been lying next to the pool for a long time, and asks the man if he wants to be healed and, if so, why the man hasn't gone into the pool. The man then reveals the challenges he has to being put into "troubled water." The individuals lying outside the pool are waiting for the water in the pool to be "troubled," to be stirred up by the flowing of the waters from the spring that feeds the pool. Moreover, they attributed such stirring of the water to divine activity; so, when one of God's messengers "troubled," or stirred up, the waters, those who stepped into the waters were healed. This final line of the refrain, then, which is repeated twice in each verse, offers a powerful image of God providing for and sustaining those who have chosen to wade into the water to find freedom. God will stir up the waters so we can hide our tracks, for God has called us to liberation, and God will protect us on our journey. Just as God called the children of Israel out of slavery in Egypt and led them across the roiling waters of the Sea of Reeds, so God calls God's children out of slavery and leads them across the turbulent waters that separate them from their freedom.

The first three verses of "Wade in the Water" take their imagery from the account of the exodus of tribes of Israelites found in Exodus 14:21–31. Throughout this biblical story, God troubles the water so that the people may flee to safety. In addition, an angel of God—which may be the basis for the "host all dressed in white" in the first verse—stands behind the people (the "host of Israel," Exod. 14:19), between them and their oppressors. God then stirs the waters, making a path between the walls of water on the people's left and right. Again, "Wade in the Water" celebrates the providence and sustenance of God, who raises up leaders to guide God's people to freedom. Just as the familiar term *children* is often used to refer to the people of Israel in Scripture, the song uses the term to refer to the people of God who are facing persecution and oppression.

The song's first verse evokes confidence and reassurance among the children who are wading in the water, for the figure that appears to them is striking—and perhaps terrifying, initially—in its dazzling brilliance and its purity: "See that host all dressed in white." This could be a reference to the angel of God mentioned in Exodus, and, if so, it creates a sense in the gathered that God is going with them on this journey, for God has sent God's messenger and protector to accompany them. It's also possible that the singer in this line refers to a gathered community that the singer envisions on the shore of a heavenly realm; in this interpretation, freedom comes when we leave this world and join the host—the many who have died before us—on that other shore. Since they are pure now—like the angels—they are dressed in white. It is also possible that those who are fleeing and wading in the water are being encouraged by a host of people on the other side of a river, or body of water, that they are crossing to freedom. The third line of the first verse refers to Moses—"The leader looks like the Israelite"—who led the people of Israel out of slavery into freedom. Drawing on these biblical images, any community singing "Wade in the Water" identifies itself immediately with the story of the people of Israel and their struggles to make their journey from slavery to freedom.

The second verse of "Wade in the Water" shifts the subject from the leaders of the movement to the community—"the band"—involved in the movement. The first line exhorts us to "see that band all dressed in red." The red clothing of the band of people contrasts with the dazzling white of the host in verse one, setting up a distinction between this human band and the divine figure of the first verse. Symbolically, the red represents the impurity of humankind and the white the purity of God. Beyond that, though, the red is also an image of the blood that this band has spilled during the years of their captivity, their enslavement. The community fleeing slavery is marked by their bloody struggles with their captors, but wading in the water will wash those stains from them as they move toward a land that promises to be without struggles. The third line in the second verse compares the community to the Israelites, and once again invokes Moses: "Looks like the band that Moses led." As with other spirituals, the genius of "Wade in the Water" is to connect the struggles of the hearers and singers of the song to the struggles described in biblical accounts that then become models of hope for this new community. Like those who followed Moses to a new land of freedom, we, also, will follow our leaders to a such a new land of hope and freedom.

The third verse of "Wade in the Water" moves from a focus on this life to a focus on the next. The first line counsels its listeners to "look over yonder," and asks them, "What do you see?" "Over yonder" could here mean "across the river" on the other banks where our people are waiting for us to help us leave this land of slavery behind. It could also mean looking beyond this world to the freedom from physical pain and suffering that awaits us in the next world, where all such pain will be absent. (As you've undoubtedly noticed by now, these images of river crossings are among the most commonly found in gospel songs and spirituals. Discovering what this means in our lives is essential for us.)

The third line of this verse answers the singer's question: "The Holy Ghost's a-coming on me." This might be the most confusing line in the song. Is the singer, like the prophet, saying that the Spirit of the Lord is upon us to utter God's words to God's people? If that is the case, is the singer then simply associating this calling with the figure of Moses—the first prophet—in the previous verse? In Isaiah 61:1, the prophet announces that "the Spirit of the LORD GOD is upon me" (the "Holy Ghost is a-coming on me," in the words of this verse), and then he goes on to say that God has anointed him to bring "liberty to the captives" and to open the "prison to those who are bound." While the singer is likely not making such a proclamation for himself, the line does illustrate the deep belief of the community that God's Spirit will accompany them and sustain them as they wade in the water to move "over yonder." Their strength comes, in part, from God's enduring guidance and love.

The final verse of "Wade in the Water" evokes another body of water that plays a central role in the history of Israel and also in the history of Christianity—the Jordan River—again with an illusion to a biblical story. In Numbers 32:29, Moses hands leadership of the people of Israel over to Joshua and the priest Eleazar and then instructs the people to prepare themselves to cross over the Jordan, where they will find homes in a new land. If we link this story of the Hebrew Old Testament—as Christians do—to the New Testament, we see that the Jordan River provides the setting for one of the Gospel of Mark's earliest stories about Jesus. Mark's Gospel tells the story of throngs of people streaming to the Jordan River to be baptized by John, the one called the Baptizer. John the Baptist is practicing a ritual washing that symbolically cleanses of impurities and sins. John's baptizing sets the stage for his baptism of Jesus in the Jordan.

Thus, this final verse of "Wade in the Water" evokes a very different kind of freedom than the song's previous verses. This verse focuses on spiritual freedom, and the progression from physical freedom to spiritual freedom illustrates the brilliance of this gospel song. As long as you're trying to throw off the yokes of your oppressors, it's hard to consider what it means to lead the Christian life or to worship God. The final verse opens with the line—"If you don't believe I've been redeemed"—and provides a response in the third line—"Just follow me down to the Jordan's stream." The singer proclaims that he's been baptized in the water that washes away his sins, and that he has been purified in that baptism. What's more significant, though, is that the singer feels a part of a redeemed community that is led by a sustaining and providing God. As such, this singer invites his hearers to experience the same freedom, love, and redemption by following him down to the river to be baptized. Wading in the water here involves a spiritual freedom that underlies the physical freedom that comes through the journey to a new land. This verse continues to remind listeners, though, that God guides in the movement to freedom, for God troubles the waters—whether in baptism or in the physical journey across the waters out of slavery.

REFLECTION

Where do we look for deliverance from our troubles and suffering? Where do we look for healing when we are in pain?

For those of us who are Christian, do we ever think about our baptism as a healing act, an act whose enduring significance provides a symbol in our lives of hope, love, and healing? When have we ever "waded in the water"? When do we "wade in the water" now in our lives? When is the last time God "troubled the water" in your life? Or in the life of your community? Perhaps you'll now look upon those troubles upon the water in a new light.

There are many versions of "Wade in the Water," from the Fisk Jubilee Singers' solemnly celebratory choral version to pop singer Eva Cassidy's bluesy acoustic version. "Wade in the Water" is a minor-chord song, so the musical structure conveys a darkness and dirgelike quality that the verses belie. Listen to several versions of "Wade in the Water," including an instrumental version such as the one by the Ramsey Lewis Trio or Herb Alpert. Choose the version that moves you the most. Why does the song move you? Which of the verses moves you the most? How does "Wade in the Water" speak to your own experience? Does the song liberate you? Does the song encourage you? Does it provide a vision of freedom for you that you wish to embrace? Do you feel the song might speak to another time and place, and so it does not speak to your own experience? How can the song speak to your own time and place?

While "Wade in the Water" reached the pinnacle of its power during the Civil Rights Movement in the 1960s, the song resonates even now for individuals and communities involved in the seeking of racial and social justice. "Wade in the Water" encourages us to bring liberation to captives, to aid those seeking freedom from the bondage of poverty or the enslavement caused by intolerance and prejudice. Singing—or listening to—"Wade in the Water" inspires hope that God can lead us to freedom from those forces that shackle us in despair; the song inspires us to make the journey to a new land, where we can embrace the beauty and possibilities that come with a new life, free from the constraints of the injustices that have bound us. Both the moving music and the lyrics of "Wade in the Water" will change your life.

Four
LEANING ON THE EVERLASTING ARMS

BACKGROUND

WHEN I WAS IN COLLEGE, I spent every Sunday in my junior and senior year playing guitar and leading the singing at the Lantana Correctional Institute, a minimum-security prison just south of West Palm Beach, Florida. Until then, I had seldom played any religious songs, having spent most of my time playing in rock bands or playing in a folk duo with a friend. When my friend, a former inmate who was going to do the teaching and preaching at these services, asked me to lead the congregational singing—and these were small congregations, as usually not more than twenty people attended our services—I wasn't convinced he had asked the right person.

However, as I sat down to practice some songs for the first Sunday, I chose three gospel songs that had been a part of my own worship experience over the years—"What a Friend We Have in Jesus," "Amazing Grace," and "Leaning on the Everlasting Arms"—because they had simple chord structures, they had an easily memorized and easily repeatable chorus, and they were moving both musically and theologically. I played other songs during those years, but I never played "A Mighty Fortress is Our God," because it just doesn't play well on guitar, and it simply is not as emotionally uplifting as the gospel songs we played.

I returned to those gospel songs so often because they wrapped the members of this little community with comfort and support that they could not find anywhere in their daily lives. The act of leaning on Jesus's arms for support and embracing Jesus as a friend who would listen to their every need filled them with hope, transforming them, at least momentarily, from individuals rejected by society to individuals precious in God's sight. "Leaning on the Everlasting Arms" especially resonated with the group because they experienced deeply the enduring promise of the security, safety, and peace that they knew grew out of their deep faith in God.

As with so many other gospel songs, "Leaning on the Everlasting Arms" was written, at least in part, in response to incomprehensible loss that required the reassurance that God would continue to provide comfort in any situation, no matter how dire. Musician Anthony Johnson Showalter and hymn writer Elisha A. Hoffman wrote "Leaning on the Everlasting Arms" in 1887. In addition to being a musician and composer, Showalter was an elder in the Presbyterian Church. Hoffman was a Presbyterian pastor.

Showalter wrote the familiar refrain—"Leaning, leaning, / Safe and secure from all alarms / Leaning, leaning, / Leaning on the everlasting arms"— to console two former pupils whose wives had died and were buried on the same day. He based his refrain on the verse from Deuteronomy 33:27, adapting it to ascribe to Jesus the role of comforter: "The eternal God is your dwelling place, and underneath are the everlasting arms." Showalter, who produced many collections of hymns and many songbooks that singing schools used in the late nineteenth and early twentieth century, also wrote the music for the song, but he asked Hoffman to help him complete it, and Hoffman finished the song by writing the verses. Hoffman, a prolific song writer with thousands of hymns attributed to him, also published songbooks, and he was the first music editor at Hope Publishing Company. Other hymns that come from his pen include "Are You Washed in the Blood?," "Down at the Cross," and "I Must Tell Jesus."

"Leaning on the Everlasting Arms" appears in many hymnals, and its simple metrical and lyrical structure—a hallmark of Hoffman's hymns—is ideal for congregation singing, which is one of the reasons the song worked so well and was so popular in my prison ministry. The song most famously appeared in James Agee's film *The Night of the Hunter* (1943) when convicted killer Robert Mitchum—with the word *love* tattooed on the knuckles of one hand and the word *hate* tattooed on the knuckles of the other—masquerading as an evangelist, sings it in the opening scene of the movie. The best-known version of the song may be Mahalia Jackson's soaring and swelling syncopated delivery of it, but it's also been recorded by country singers Alan Jackson and George Jones and Christian singers Twila Paris and Selah, among many others.

"LEANING ON THE EVERLASTING ARMS"

"Leaning on the Everlasting Arms" is a jubilant, rhythmic gospel song that moves congregations. This song creates joy; congregations smile when they sing it since they are moved mightily by the reassurance it offers. It is sung often at tent revivals and camp meetings, where quartets or choirs will encourage audiences to clap their hands and stomp their feet and to rejoice in wonder at the goodness of God as God provides continual comfort, everywhere and always, for God's people, if they will lean on God.

The poetic structure of "Leaning on the Everlasting Arms," as with the poetic structure of other gospel songs, makes it easy for audiences to sing along, and the tune is memorable enough that individuals will be humming it to themselves long after the service is finished. "Leaning on the Everlasting Arms" is a gospel song that lives within you, always offering rest and reflection and reassurance. The song is easy to remember, too, because there are only two lines, which rhyme, followed by a portion of the refrain in each verse, and the song contains only three verses. So, the first line of the first verse is "What a fellowship, what a joy divine / Leaning on the everlasting arms." Such lyrical structure also creates an opportunity for singers and choirs and congregations to sing the song in a modified call-and-response fashion. An alternate refrain can be sung by the basses in a choir or quartet, adding some choral complexity to the song. The alternate refrain floats underneath the first words of the main refrain with the phrase "leaning on Jesus, leaning on Jesus."

The first verse sets the joyous tone for the song, rejoicing in the community that surrounds the singer: "What a fellowship, what a joy divine." *Divine* describes not only the everlasting, or eternally enduring, community of the saints that surround everyone in the community singing the song; it also tries to name the indescribable, ineffable joy that grows out of being a part of a community of saints who have gone on before us to the heavenly realm. The jubilation of being a part of this divine fellowship ushers in a blessedness and peace that the singer embraces: "What a blessedness, what a peace is mine." In other words, the singer knows that no matter what kinds of loss or disappointments or defeats that he faces in life—even if he faces the death of a loved one—he can find peace in knowing that he's an intimate part of this divine fellowship. In fact, the singer owns this peace—"what a peace is mine"—because the singer inhabits this community. The singer never has to wonder again if he has peace once he affirms his place in the community.

The second verse of "Leaning on the Everlasting Arms" is all sweetness and light. As the singer journeys through life, he embarks on this journey from a secure place where he is loved and cherished. The singer is a pilgrim, always searching for truth, meaning, comfort, and hope in this world and, also, on his journey to the next. It is "sweet to walk in this pilgrim way," says the singer, because the path is precious and filled with signs of God's wonder and grace. It is also satisfying to make this pilgrimage because of all those who have walked this way before, leaving markers of their own experiences to help guide the way. Not only is the journey satisfying, but "the path grows" bright "from day to day"; God is always providing the light that illumines the path of the journey. The path also grows brighter every day, though, because the pilgrim draws closer and closer to God's face, and nearer and nearer to seeing God's brilliance face-to-face. There is a light toward which the pilgrim continues to walk, drawn by the promise of everlasting blessedness and peace and upheld by the divine fellowship and the communion of the saints.

In the third verse, the singer boldly asks, "What have I to dread, what have I to fear?" The assurances of the previous two verses lead naturally to the singer's opening questions of the final verse, for the encircling love of a community, the brilliance that marks the singer's path to God, and the sweetness of the spiritual joy of leaning on God's everlasting presence give the speaker confidence and assurance. Yet the questions in the opening lines are also answered by the last line of the final verse: "I have blessed peace with my Lord so near." God draws near to the singer in the blessed fellowship of the community; God hovers near as the singer traverses the rugged landscape of this life in search of peace and spiritual meaning. God illumines the pilgrim's path. God is always near, the song indicates, and the blessed peace comes from the feeling that the singer has that God never distances God's self from those who embrace God's way. The peace also comes from knowing that the singer is close to seeing God face-to-face, as well as in knowing that the path he is on will lead to the peacefulness of God's heavenly kingdom.

The refrain bolsters and encourages the singer. "Leaning" is an active measure that keeps us safe from all dangers—"safe and secure from all alarms"—but we only lean when we have a substance on which we can lean. "Leaning on the Everlasting Arms" promises that God will always be there to hold us up, to provide a place where we can rest our heads, to light our way as we travel in search of meaning, to offer comfort when fears and anxieties surround us, and to help create a loving and just community that always provides a place for any of us—even the strangers among us—to lay our heads and be safe and secure.

REFLECTION

Do you have trials and tribulations? Is there trouble in your life? Are you discouraged? Has a friend or loved one died recently? Or does the memory of the death of a loved one remain lodged in your heart so that you are unable to move past it to embrace and celebrate the joy of that individual's life? Do you feel marginalized in your church community? Are you without church, and wishing it was otherwise? Do you feel distant from God? Do you feel as if you will never find peace and blessedness and that you will always struggle to find a spiritual identity? Do you feel as if you simply can't find your way spiritually?

"Leaning on the Everlasting Arms" is an uplifting gospel song that invites us to celebrate and embrace our spiritual community. It urges us to recognize our place among the divine fellowship of our fellow believers and to join them in walking on the pilgrim way that carries us toward God. "Leaning on the Everlasting Arms" offers the promise that we are never alone on our search for God, spiritual identity, and joyful community. The gospel song jubilantly praises God's presence in our lives, encouraging us to remember that God sustains and provides even when life is the darkest.

Listen to Mahalia Jackson's version of "Leaning on the Everlasting Arms." Close your eyes and listen just to the music the first and second time you listen to the song; then listen again to the song, but this time listen carefully to the lyrics. Reflect on the ways that the music moves you. Is the music alone transformative? Do you need the lyrics to complete your emotional response to the song? Listen to other versions of "Leaning on the Everlasting Arms," and reflect on them in the same ways. When is the last time you sang "Leaning on the Everlasting Arms" in church, or in any setting, and do you recall the occasion for singing it? Do you recall how you felt when you sang it?

Most of all, "Leaning on the Everlasting Arms" affirms that we are never alone. With its combination of rousing music and joyous, life-affirming lyrics, "Leaning on the Everlasting Arms" reassures us that the divine fellowship of the communion of saints that surrounds us helps us make our journey through life by lighting our way and helping us see the path to God. This is why "Leaning on the Everlasting Arms" can change your life.

FIVE
SWING LOW,
SWEET CHARIOT

BACKGROUND

WHILE MANY OF US MIGHT routinely pick up our hymnals and sing along with the choir director or song leader when "Swing Low, Sweet Chariot" comes up in our congregations, we now have the opportunity to listen to versions of the traditional spiritual that are so surprising that we find new meanings in the song. For example, rhythm and blues and rap singer Beyoncé delivers a version of the song that focuses on the power of home and our yearning for it. She brilliantly punctuates the tune of the spiritual with the strains of an old rock song, "Rock Me Baby," and then she proceeds in sing-song fashion to repeat: "I got a home / You got a home / We got a home." It's a stunning rendition of the song that makes you stop for a minute to consider fresh significance for a song that is, for many, perhaps too familiar.

As with many spirituals, the origins of "Swing Low, Sweet Chariot" are somewhat uncertain. It's very likely a traditional spiritual that was passed down orally among slaves who first sang it as a call-and-response field shout. Calling out verses about the vision of a chariot of God and a band of angels coming to carry them away to a different home, these slaves could conceal their anger with their place in life while at the same time shouting out the hope for a much different life in a better place. Like other spirituals, "Swing Low, Sweet Chariot" may have contained coded messages about escape and instructions about ways of escape that the slaves could understand but which their owners could not. As long as the songs the slaves were singing were about God and heaven, the slaves' owners had little to fear from the slaves who were working on their property. Because "Swing Low, Sweet Chariot" can be sung as a song with codes about escape to the North on routes along the Underground Railroad, this song also has sometimes been attributed to abolitionist Harriet Tubman (just like "Wade in the Water").

"Swing Low, Sweet Chariot" has also been attributed to Wallace Willis, who was born in Mississippi, but who became the slave of an owner who was at least half-Choctaw. When this owner was forced to move to the Oklahoma Territory, he took Willis and Willis's wife with him, where they worked in a boys' school called Spencer Academy, where Willis began to compose and to sing music. According to this story of origin, a minister at the Spencer Academy, Alexander Reid, heard Willis singing the song, wrote it out, and gave it to the Fisk Jubilee Singers to carry with them on their 1871 concert tour.

The song was collected in the 1867 songbook *Slave Songs of the United States*, put together by William F. Allen, Charles Ware, and Lucy McKim Garrison, so some version of "Swing Low, Sweet Chariot" may have been circulating orally prior to Willis's version of it. The Fisk Jubilee Singers made the earliest recording of the spiritual in 1909, and since then artists ranging from Eric Clapton, Sam Cooke, Peggy Lee, and Bing Crosby to Etta James, Josh Turner, and Beyoncé have recorded it.

"SWING LOW, SWEET CHARIOT"

Like many other spirituals, "Swing Low, Sweet Chariot" conveys a yearning for freedom, and like other spirituals it also looks beyond this world to find the hope of such freedom. The central themes of this popular gospel song are home, community, and freedom, and the lyrics express these themes by weaving biblical imagery—notice how a tour of gospel songs inevitably involves discovering various themes from the Bible—through the lines of the urgent longing to be carried away to a place where the singers can be united with family and friends. As with other spirituals, "Swing Low, Sweet Chariot" could have provided coded messages to slaves seeking to be transported away from slaveholders to a new home in a free land, joining others who had gone ahead to make a place for them. At the same time, "Swing Low, Sweet Chariot" depicts a heavenly home, "across the Jordan" where "bands of angels" gather and fly to the aid of the suffering and oppressed, gathering them in "chariots" to "carry them home." To cross the river Jordan was to find freedom, first in this world, then the next. The Jordan River occurs again and again in gospels and spirituals.

"Swing Low, Sweet Chariot" flows musically along a call-and-response stream, with the last two lines of the refrain—"coming for to carry me home"—repeated as the response to the called-out lines of each verse. Although we sing this spiritual in churches or at revival meetings these days, the earliest versions of "Swing Low, Sweet Chariot" would likely have been those field shouts or hollers, again, with one person moaning the main line and then others joining in by repeating the refrain as the shout echoed across the field. One person would thus call out a line such as "I looked over Jordan, what did I see," and the others would shout out "coming for to carry me home" in response. Imagine this as a way of singing the song, today.

The refrain itself conveys the welcoming sight of a mode of transportation—"sweet chariot"—that has arrived to carry the singer away to his long-desired home. If the spiritual contains a coded message for slaves seeking to escape along the route of the Underground Railroad, the "chariot" is an image of that "railroad." The request for the chariot to "swing low" would be a plea for the network of safe routes for escape to come down into all the places, especially the southern states, out of which slaves yearned to be carried away. The chariot then carries the singer home, or to a safe place across the Ohio River or perhaps the St. Croix River, the Niagara River, or any of the crossover points from the United States into Canada.

At the same time, "Swing Low, Sweet Chariot" expresses a desire to be carried away to a heavenly home, safe from all the travails of this world. The chariot in the refrain evokes the image of the chariot in the Old Testament book of 2 Kings 3:11—"the chariots of Israel and its horsemen"—that transported Elijah to the side of God, as he went up to heaven in a whirlwind, as well as the image of God's chariots in Psalm 68. In that psalm, God delivers God's people in God's "mighty chariotry," much in the same way that the singers of the spiritual plea for deliverance from their own captivity. The plea for the chariot to "swing low" is a plea simply for God to come down from heaven with

God's chariot to carry the captives "home." "Home," in this case, is a place in heaven filled with family and friends and where a benevolent God—and not a malevolent slaveholder—reigns in love and peace. The home of the spiritual is idyllic, as compared to the dreadful environment of the singers' earthly home, where families are torn apart, never to be reunited.

In the first verse of "Swing Low, Sweet Chariot," the singers gaze longingly at another place that is beyond their present home: "I looked over Jordan, what did I see?" The singers would have been very familiar with the biblical stories of the Israelites crossing the Jordan River (Num. 32:29) and God's leading them to their new home. Here, the singers cast their glances across the bodies of water that separate them from freedom. If "Swing Low, Sweet Chariot" contains coded messages for slaves, then looking over Jordan could mean "looking" over specific rivers or bodies of water toward a land where the "chariot" could carry you. On the other hand, crossing the Jordan could be symbolic of crossing into a new heavenly home, especially if the third line in this first verse that refers to a "band of angels" is taken as a literal response to the question asked in the first line: "What did I see?" The third line of the first verse responds to the question in the first line, shouting out that the singers see "a band of angels coming after me."

In the coded message of the spiritual, the band of angels would be the workers within the network of the Underground Railroad. These workers are "coming after me": they've not forgotten those enslaved or their families and are coming to carry them to a safe haven. In the spiritual reading, the "band of angels" is literally a group of angels—the hosts of heaven—swinging low in God's chariot to come get the oppressed and carry them to their heavenly home.

The second verse of "Swing Low, Sweet Chariot" evokes a community that the singers look forward to joining. The singer tells his families and friends that if they "get there before I do," to let them know that "I'm coming, too." This second verse illustrates the enduring value of community; even in a world of suffering and oppression and want, individuals draw their power from being in community and sharing their hopes with one another. Too often communities and families were torn apart violently—either through separating children from parents or separating husbands and wives or through gruesome deaths by whipping or lynching—and often never saw each other again. The promise of being together again in a new home and being carried there by a "band of angels" across the Ohio River was a fervent hope of individuals and communities. Thus, when others reached that new home on the other side of the river, they were counseled to remember those who had been left behind and to spread the word that those left behind would soon be joining them. From a spiritual perspective, the friends who have gone on to heaven before others in their community become those who petition for those left behind, keeping them in their memory and in the presence of God. Some versions of "Sweet Low, Sweet Chariot" contain a variation on this verse that promises that "if I get there before you do / I'll cut a hole and pull you through."

The third and fourth verses of "Swing Low, Sweet Chariot" turn more personal and focus more on individual redemption than on the salvation or the transformation of a community. The response, "Coming for to carry me home," floats through each of these verses, providing the lyrical thread that ties together the entire song. The third verse depicts the spiritual ambivalence of the singers—"I'm sometimes up, I'm sometimes down"—but despite such ambivalence the singers nevertheless affirm that their "soul feels heavenly bound." Read as coded message, the verse continues to express the singers' hope that they can make the journey on the Underground Railroad—"heavenly bound"— despite their daily tribulations. Read from a spiritual perspective, the verse radiates the singers' confidence that, despite the physical and spiritual trials of this world, as long as they have a strong relationship with Jesus, their souls are bound to be transported to a heavenly home in which there will be no more ups and downs. The song's final verse underscores the spiritual confidence of the third verse, offering the reason for the singers' optimism about their souls being bound for heaven: "The brightest day that I can say / When Jesus washed my sins away."

REFLECTION

How can a song that sings of chariots swinging low have any meaning for us today? What does it even mean to "swing low"? What does a song about a "band of angels coming after me" mean for us? Can "Swing Low, Sweet Chariot" provide hope or joy in our present circumstances?

There are many versions of "Swing Low, Sweet Chariot" available, ranging from the first recording by the Fisk Jubilee Singers to a rocking rhythm and blues version by Beyoncé. Listen to several versions of "Swing Low, Sweet Chariot," paying close attention to the ways that the song opens, the ways it builds to its climax, and the ways it closes. Some versions begin slowly and then blossom into a syncopated jazz; others open with spare vocals and ascend into a lively choral call and response. Which of these versions moves you the most? Why does it move you? Do the lyrics, which you might not feel relate to your own life, move you? Do they provide you with insight into your own life and faith? Does the music move you? What about the music moves you? Does the music transport you, like the chariot, carrying you to spiritual heights you never dreamed of reaching? Does the music so move you that you feel as if you've been carried home? If so, the music has reached down to you—"swung low"—and been your chariot to carry you away home.

"Swing Low, Sweet Chariot" offers a dazzling vision of a life beyond the spiritual ups and downs we experience in this life. The spiritual offers us hope that God can deliver us, carry us, to a new home where we'll no longer experience oppression, suffering, or violence. The spiritual also praises the creation of a community where our families and friends will be together with us and no longer fear being broken apart. Such communities of enduring relationships, where peace and justice are valued among its members, can also become for us that place "across the Jordan." When we sing "Swing Low, Sweet Chariot," we are petitioning God to carry us into this new community, to this new home, and far beyond the social, political, religious, and personal ups and downs of the world in which we live. For these reasons, "Swing Low, Sweet Chariot" is a spiritual that can change your life.

SIX
WILL THE CIRCLE
BE UNBROKEN?

MANY PEOPLE WILL BE FAMILIAR with the country folk ballad "Will the Circle Be Unbroken?"—not from singing it in church, but from hearing it performed by George Jones, the Avett Brothers, or the Nitty Gritty Dirt Band, whose version—which can be found on their 1972 album of the same name—probably remains the best known of modern versions. Rock singer Gregg Allman also included it on his first solo album, *Laid Back* (1973), and Leon Russell, Bob Dylan and the Band, and the Staple Singers have all delivered their own versions. Arrangements of the song vary, as well, from Allman's slow, pensive, downright mournful blues to the Staple's heart-rending, soul-shouting gospel take on the song. As in many other gospel songs, the subject of "Will the Circle Be Unbroken?" is death and mourning, and this song includes lyrics that describe the narrator's feelings at his mother's funeral.

Although "Will the Circle Be Unbroken?" is most often attributed to A. P. Carter, the scion of the musical Carter Family—whose songs, written by various members of the family, such as "Wildwood Flower" and "Keep on the Sunny Side," are some of the most memorable in American music—in fact it was Ada Ruth Habershon who composed the song in 1907. In the late nineteenth century, Habershon—an accomplished lecturer on biblical topics and a hymn writer—met Ira Sankey, the hymn leader for Dwight L. Moody's evangelistic crusades. Habershon started writing hymns in the early twentieth century and contributed several hundred to Charles Alexander, an east Tennessee native who served as song leader for evangelist R. A. Torrey (who succeeded D. L. Moody as leader of the Bible school Moody founded in Chicago).

Habershon wrote the lyrics for "Will the Circle Be Unbroken?," and the prolific hymn writer Charles H. Gabriel composed the tune. Gabriel published several songbooks of hymns. Either the lyrics or tunes of such familiar gospel songs and hymns as "Brighten the Corner Where You Are" (perhaps the most famous), "Send the Light," "Since Jesus Came into My Heart," and "His Eye Is on the Sparrow" come from his hand. Except for the chorus, Habershon's original sounds unfamiliar to most listeners, who are more familiar with A. P. Carter's later reworking of the song to give it a more immediate and intimate character.

A. P. (Alvin Pleasant) Carter was born into a strict religious home in Scott County, Virginia, in the southwest corner of the state. He grew up with a love of religious music, but he also acquired a love for the sound of the fiddle, which he heard played by various individuals around his community. As the story goes, Carter's parents called the fiddle the devil's music, but that didn't stop Carter from working hard to earn his own money to acquire one. Carter fell in love with one of his neighbors, Sara Dougherty, who had a beautiful singing voice, and the two soon married. Maybelle Addington, who played autoharp, banjo, and guitar, married A. P.'s brother, Ezra, and the four of them started playing music in and around their community as the Carter Family. In 1927, the Carter Family went to Bristol, Tennessee, where producer Ralph Peer recorded several sessions of their music. While the group played many of A. P.'s originals, they also played versions of traditional ballads or songs that Peer brought to them to sing. Among those songs was "Will the Circle Be Unbroken?" The family revised the lyrics of Habershorn's original, and Sara's and Maybelle's singing, as well as the latter's distinctive guitar licks and autoharp riffs, give the song its distinctive and familiar flavor. The Carter Family's version captures the aching heart of a singer whose mother has died and who looks with longing to being reunited with her in a blissful state of wholeness, where they'll never again be parted by death.

"WILL THE CIRCLE BE UNBROKEN?"

Artists and audiences often gather to sing "Will the Circle Be Unbroken?" as a valedictory anthem. The crowd joins hands and sways to the languorous piano or stealthily plucked banjo or rolling guitar as the singers lead a sing-along. The song creates a momentary feeling of unity among the crowd, consoling them that they'll meet the band again at its next area concert and promoting musical and social solidarity.

The song's chorus is familiar: "Will the circle be unbroken / By and by, Lord, by and by / There's a better home a-waiting / In the sky, Lord, in the sky." As the audience sings along, they seldom hear the references to religion in the verses and in the chorus. Many audiences think of this as a joyful song—and it is joyful, in its own way—and sing lustily about the circle of friendship or music that they hope will never be broken, at least in their lives. They hear the words as a call to hope that the moments they now experience as a community—or perhaps as a family—will return to them again in an unbroken continuum of love and friendship. When the Nitty Gritty Dirt Band recorded its now-iconic album *Will the Circle Be Unbroken?* in 1971, for example, they were trying to bring two arcs of the circle of country and folk music together: the jug band and contemporary country of a younger generation of musicians—the Nitty Gritty Dirt Band—and an older generation of country musicians, many of them folk musicians from Appalachia, including Mother Maybelle Carter—the sister-in-law of A.P. Carter—Doc Watson, and Merle Travis, among others.

Yet when we listen closely to the lyrics of "Will the Circle Be Unbroken?," we discover that it's not such a joyful song after all, nor is it a sentimental song about the unbroken circle of music that can transform our lives. "Will the Circle Be Unbroken?" depicts the death of a loved one, the accompanying of the body in a funeral procession, and the haunting question of whether or not the singer—given the promises he or she has heard about being reunited with loved ones in heaven—will meet his loved one in a better world in the sky and be reunited with him or her. The Carter Family's version, titled "Can the Circle Be Unbroken?," is much more immediate, intimate, and personal than Habershon's original, which offers a less personal and more idealized view of the circle of loved ones reuniting in heaven: "There are loved ones in the glory / Will you join them in their bliss?"

The chorus of Habershon's song features the now-familiar questions that the song's narrator asks about reuniting with loved ones in a new world: "Will the circle be unbroken / By and by, by and by / Is a better home awaiting / In the sky, in the sky?" The song not only asks whether the circle of love broken by death and loss will be restored, but it ponders—unlike the Carter version— whether there is indeed a better home waiting for us. The more well-known words of the Carter version affirm that there is such a place in the sky—"There's a better home a-waiting"—where the ones who are waiting to join departed loved ones will be rewarded with reunion.

Often didactic and moralistic, Habershon's song often sounds unsettling and scary to modern ears. The "dear forms" that once inhabited the family's sitting room have now left behind empty seats as they have traveled to "glory." Habershon's version draws a portrait of a world clearly separated between the earthly realm and the heavenly realm, which is depicted as residing in the sky. To enter the heavenly realm, according to the song, we must have listened to the stories of the "dying Savior" that our dearly departed ones told us about and embrace the truths of those stories. The song reminds us that those who have left us reside in the arms of the "dying Savior" and portrays the gatherings of these loved ones as happy.

The opening verse of Habershon's song asks whether or not we will join our loved ones; we have a choice, the song reminds us, and words such as *dear*, *loved*, *glory*, and *bliss* convey the beauty of the world that we can choose to enter if we decide to follow the ways of Jesus and not the ways of the world. The first two lines evoke the absence of our loved ones and their new home in glory—"There are loved ones in the glory / Whose dear forms you often miss." The last two lines of the opening verse starkly pose the question about where we wish to spend our eternal future: "When you close your earthly story / Will you join them in their bliss?" In just this one verse, the evangelistic tenor of the song is established, and this tone persists through the rest of the verses. As if to urge those left behind to be sure that they'll secure a place for themselves among their dear ones in the blissful realm, the song contrasts the tearfulness of this world with the happiness and joy of the better world awaiting in the sky.

The final two verses of the song offer an idealized picture of the better world and ask directly if one day we will complete the broken circle by joining this world. The penultimate verse contrasts the exalted character of the next world and the emptiness of this world: "You can picture happy gatherings / Round the fireside long ago / And you think of tearful partings / When they left you here below." The final verse opens almost like a ghost story, with souls flying away to this idyllic world, and closes by asking us whether we'll join this now-departed family: "One by one their seats were emptied / One by one they went away / Now the family is parted / Will it be complete one day?"

The third verse may be the most interesting, since it contrasts the beauty and meaning of hymns and sacred music with secular music. The verse implies that in our choice to sing earthly songs, we are making a decision not to join our dearly departed ones in "the glory" and to complete the circle that death has broken. The verse also illustrates that the faith we learn as children is the faith that we can cherish and embrace all our lives, and it is the faith that informs our choices as we grow older: "You remember songs of heaven / Which you sang with childish voice / Do you love the hymns they taught you? / Or are the songs of earth your choice?" After the starkness of this verse, the song's chorus asks once again if there is a better home waiting for us, and if we will break the circle or if the circle will be unbroken.

The Carter Family version, "Can the Circle Be Unbroken?," delivers a more poignant picture of loss and the desire to be reunited in a world where death has lost its sting. In contrast to the original version, "Can the Circle Be Unbroken?" speaks in the first person instead of the third person, so we can identify with an individual who has experienced the pain that comes with the death of a loved one and the excruciating loneliness that follows an attempt to return home and to a normal life. The verses build layer by layer as the speaker tells a story of watching the hearse come to pick up his mother's body from the home where she has died. In the rural South, many individuals would have sat with their loved ones' bodies overnight and prepared their bodies for burial. In some cases, these individuals would have built caskets for their departed family members and would have transported them in a wooden farm wagon to a freshly dug grave, either on their property or in a small cemetery at their church. In this case, the speaker is watching the hearse coming to pick up his mother to carry her away. Notice how this verse sets the tone for the song: it's a "cold and cloudy day," and that darkness never lets up in the entire song. In fact, the only glimmer of light in the song is the third line in the chorus, which affirms—where Habershon's poses a question—that "there's a better home a-waiting / In the sky, Lord, in the sky." Notice, also, the inexorable slowness of the funerary activities in the song: the hearse comes "rolling," taking its time, and the speaker pleads with the "undertaker [to] please drive slow," for the speaker "hate[s] to see [his mother] go."

The Carter Family's version of "Will the Circle Be Unbroken?" also offers a portrait of brokenness that Habershon's version lacks. Here, we witness the speaker following as close as he can to his mother—it's the hearse carrying his mother's casket that he's following, but notice that he personalizes the verse: just as in life he followed "close behind her," so he does the same in death—since he hates to see her go. The speaker tries to "be brave" and to hold his emotions in check, but he cannot control himself when they bury his mother: "I could not hide my sorrow / When they laid her in the grave." The grief of laying his mother in her grave is only the beginning of the speaker's sorrow, though, for when he gets home, his "home was lonesome"; he misses his mother, and his brothers and sisters are also crying inconsolably. This one verse contrasts the desolate emptiness—"mother . . . was gone"; "home [was] so sad and lone"—of his home with the joyous full-ness of the better world that awaits his mother—and eventually his family—in the sky.

The final verse of the Carter Family version offers a beautiful twist on the third verse. In the original, choosing to sing hymns is set in contrast to choosing to sing earthly songs, and heavenly reward depends on choosing hymns over earthly songs. The final verse of the Carter Family song doesn't ask us to make a choice; rather, the speaker affirms that his loneliness can be overcome, his momentary sadness redeemed, and his vision of a better world affirmed by singing the "hymns of faith that made us strong." As the family gathers at the sad and lonesome home, they console each other with music: "We sang the songs of childhood / Hymns of faith that made us strong / Ones that mother Maybelle taught us / Hear the angels sing along." If there is one verse in all of gospel music that affirms the redemptive power of music and the transformative character of music, this is it. The song then ends with the chorus, which confirms that the circle of family love will be restored once again in a better home waiting in the sky.

REFLECTION

What happens after our loved ones die? Do they fly away to a better world in the sky? Can we join them when we die? How do we know that our loved ones occupy a place in a better world waiting in the sky? What does such a world look like? Will the circle of our family—a circle broken by death—really be made whole again? Do our hopes reside in the promise of a better world in the sky? Are we looking beyond our world to a better world beyond, and can we find healing in such a vision? There has never been a human being alive who did not ponder one or more of these questions.

"Will the Circle Be Unbroken?" raises all these questions in an emotional and heartrending fashion. The musical structure of the various versions of the songs builds slowly, mimicking the rolling movement of the hearse and its slow ride to the cemetery. Most modern versions of the Carter Family song, with the exception of the Nitty Gritty Dirt Band version, develop around gospel-inflected vocals or swelling piano chords, drawing us into the hope for restoration, for seeing our families once again, for living in community with those loved ones we dearly miss in a better world.

Who among us has not returned from the funeral of a loved one to an empty home and felt the sadness brought on by our loved one's absence? Who among us has not wanted a memorial service or funeral not to end because we know that when the service ends we face the finality of never seeing our loved one again? Who among us finds comfort in hoping that a better world exists in which the finality of death is not indeed the end, but there is a world in which we'll join our loved ones in the glory? Does such a world exist? Are there any promises that such a better world exists? Music can help us understand these things.

"Will the Circle Be Unbroken?" embraces the vision of such a world and offers hope for those aching from the pain and loss of death. Despite its mournful quality, there is a jubilant quality to the song that promises transformation and the hope of reuniting with our loved ones.

Choose several versions of "Will the Circle Be Unbroken?," and listen to them closely. What is your reaction to each one? How does each song engage your emotions? What are the ways that these versions evoke joy or sadness? Which version helps you to transform your loneliness into community, your sadness into joy, your disappointment into hope? Which version of "Will the Circle Be Unbroken?" changes your life?

SEVEN
KEEP YOUR LAMPS TRIMMED AND BURNING

BACKGROUND

A FEW YEARS AGO, Larry Campbell and Teresa Williams—the husband-and-wife duo who played and sang for several years with Levon Helm, the former drummer of The Band—opened their set with their version of the old gospel song "Keep Your Lamps Trimmed and Burning." The moment started quietly enough with Larry Campbell's chicken-picked guitar in his slow blues slide through an instrumental intro before Teresa Williams's soaring vocals carried the song higher and higher, transporting the audience to a new plane of existence.

The song has a simple call-and-response musical structure, with a minimum of four verses and a chorus. With their version, Campbell and Williams deliver a powerful anointing. Williams's soulful shouting carries the tune. She preaches and testifies in her singing, propelled by Campbell's driving electric blues guitar. The climax of the song comes in the final line—"for this old world is almost done"—as Williams holds the word *almost* for two bars before sliding down into the final word *done*. In the performance of "Keep Your Lamps Trimmed and Burning," the duo elevated the audience, leaving them breathless and transforming an ordinary moment into a moment that transcended time and place.

Campbell and Williams performed their version of the song based on the one that Reverend Gary Davis introduced to numerous musicians in New York—from the Soul Stirrers to the Staple Singers and Jorma Kaukonen and Campbell—in the folk revival of the 1960s, when many musicians recognized spirituals and blues as an integral part of the American folk tradition. Davis, who was born in Laurens, South Carolina, started playing blues guitar and banjo as a way of escaping the troubles of this world. He developed a unique thumb-picked guitar style that he would later teach those who studied with him, including Campbell, Kaukonen, and folk blues musician David Bromberg, among others. In the late 1930s, Davis converted to Christianity and became ordained as a Baptist preacher. He turned then to playing gospel music, but his songs, or versions of earlier spirituals, retained their blues inflections. Davis recorded his version of "Keep Your Lamps Trimmed and Burning" in the mid-1950s, and his version is credited to him on an album called *American Street Songs*.

While Davis is most often credited for the song, the real composer of "Keep Your Lamps Trimmed and Burning" was a Texas blues and gospel musician named Blind Willie Johnson, whose deep, gravelly voice and acoustic-slide guitar playing influenced several blues guitarists, including Davis. Blind Willie Johnson was a blues-gospel musical artist, and an evangelist, born in Texas in 1897. He wrote and recorded thirty songs in the early decades of the twentieth century in a little studio in the famous Deep Ellum neighborhood of Dallas—the rough-and-tumble section of town immortalized in the Lone Star Cowboys' song "Deep Ellum Blues." Many of Johnson's songs have become well known through versions recorded by artists ranging from Bob Dylan to Led Zeppelin to Eric Clapton.

The titles of many of Johnson's songs depict the struggle that many Christians experience between the temptations of living solely to gratify bodily pleasures and the rewards of leading a spiritual life: "Dark Was the Night, Cold Was the Ground," "Lord, I Just Can't Keep from Crying," "I Know His Blood Can Make Me Whole." Johnson's apocalyptic fervor shines through in the titles of many of his songs: "If I Had My Way I'd Tear the Building Down," "Jesus Is Coming Soon," "Jesus Make Up My Dying Bed," "John the Revelator," and "Keep Your Lamps Trimmed and Burning." In his powerful, raspy voice, Johnson thunders the message of redemption from the waywardness of sinfulness, and he exhorts watchfulness and readiness for the return of Jesus to redeem this world. While lyrics in the verses vary slightly in various versions of the song, Johnson's refrain— "keep your lamps trimmed and burning"—remains the song's centerpiece, with the verses circling around it, emphasizing the thematic force of the refrain.

"KEEP YOUR LAMPS TRIMMED AND BURNING"

Although Campbell and Williams recorded "Keep Your Lamps Trimmed and Burning" on their debut album in 2016, several other artists, from rock to folk to bluegrass musicians, have included their own version of this spiritual on their albums over the past forty years. Perhaps the most famous modern version belongs to Jorma Kaukonen, the guitarist who was one of the founders of the Jefferson Airplane and Hot Tuna and who included the song on a Hot Tuna album in 1971. Kaukonen once told me he learned the song from the Reverend Gary Davis, the Piedmont blues musician who is given credit for writing a shorter version of the original that balances the musical structure of the blues with the musical structure of gospel. Campbell admits that the first time he heard Reverend Gary Davis's "Keep Your Lamp Trimmed and Burning," he was terrified trying to follow Davis's playing. Then he heard Kaukonen's interpretation of the song. "After I listened to Jorma," he recalls, "I went back to Reverend Gary Davis, and I understood that song."

Like many other gospel songs, "Keep Your Lamps Trimmed and Burning" focuses on specific themes that will resonate with Christians almost immediately, even as its haunting music and metrical and lyrical repetition entrances listeners outside of any religious community. Its musical foundation is the blues, and this particular song illustrates better than many other gospel songs the close family connection of the blues and spirituals. As Campbell and Williams's version demonstrates, the song evokes a world-weariness that cries out to be overcome, even as their version mimics the encouragement and hope that waiting for a new order brings: "this old world is almost done!" That one line beautifully captures the hope inherent in the weariness: the old and tired world, as well as an individual's weariness of living in a world that continues to oppress him or her for the color of his or her skin, is almost done; a new day is dawning; wait for it and rejoice! There is hope and power in the waiting. On that night when Campbell and Williams performed the song, the audience consisted of a wide range of individuals—some religious and some nonreligious—but when the duo finished their song, everyone had been redeemed.

"Keep Your Lamps Trimmed and Burning" draws its subject matter from the Gospel of Matthew 25:1–13, a parable known in the Christian traditions as the Tale of the Ten Virgins, the Parable of the Wise and Foolish Virgins, or the Parable of the Ten Bridesmaids. The multiple names are probably testimony to the multiplicity of meaning in this short passage from the teachings of Jesus. In the parable, ten women take their oil lamps and go out to await the arrival of a bridegroom. Five of the virgins carry enough oil to keep their lamps burning, but the other five do not carry enough oil to keep their lamps burning. The story depicts the women waiting a lengthy time for the groom to arrive—long enough for each group of women to fall asleep. When the groom arrives, someone wakes the women and exhorts them to go out to meet him. The bridesmaids rise to trim their lamps; the women who have brought enough oil are able to light their lamps and go out to meet the groom, but the women who have not brought enough oil implore the others to share their oil with them. The bridesmaids who have enough oil refuse to share their oil, sending the others to vendors so that they can buy more and replenish their supplies. While these five women go to buy oil, the groom arrives, and the women who were ready for him accompany him into the wedding. The other five women return with oil in their lamps but find the doors to the wedding closed to them. When these women implore the groom to allow them to join the party, he refuses to acknowledge them. The moral of the parable is to be prepared—"keep your lamps trimmed and burning"—for no one knows when the groom (the spiritual implication is that this is Jesus, to whom they are to be spiritually espoused) will come to usher in the kingdom of heaven. Those who first heard the parable expected "this old world to be almost done," in the words of the song, soon and in their lifetime, and the parable counsels that wisdom—being ready—erases worries and anxieties about entering the kingdom of heaven. Johnson, Mississippi Fred McDowell, and Reverend Gary Davis each focus on the ways individuals can act to gain comfort in being prepared for the world to be done.

The persistent themes of "Keep Your Lamps Trimmed and Burning" are weariness with the world in which we now live and hope for the coming of a new world where we'll no longer be tired and weary. Every version of the song counsels us not to be "worried," for our journey here will soon be over, and we'll soon reach heaven. Every version of the song focuses on the nearness of that time when the new world will come, and each version encourages us not to stop praying or preaching or preparing ourselves for the coming of this new world.

In the chorus of Blind Willie Johnson's version—which repeats the refrain from which the song gets its title—the last line is "O, see what the Lord has done." The final line of the verses, which function as responses to the refrain, focuses on our labors in this world: "for the work is almost done." In Reverend Gary Davis's version, the last line of the verses is "for this old world is almost done," a variation that focuses not on our work but on the hopefulness that grows out of the coming end of this tired old world in which we live. Other versions of the song close the chorus and the verses with a slight variation on Davis's version: "for the time is drawing nigh." Each version conveys the sense that this realm will be ending soon and that the "Christian's journey"—as one version puts it—will soon be over, so Christians should not be worried, for that time is almost here.

Each verse of Davis's version of "Keep Your Lamps Trimmed and Burning" calls out specific groups of people as it shouts encouragement to be prepared. In the first verse, the song exhorts brothers not to worry; the second verse exhorts sisters to keep praying ("don't stop praying"); the third verse urges fathers not to worry; in the fourth and climactic verse, the song urges preachers not to stop preaching ("don't stop your preaching"). Scattered through other versions of the song are references to "darker midnight" lying before us, and the "morning soon breaking." Such images reflect the apocalyptic tone of the book of Revelation, as well as the apocalyptic parables of the Gospel of Matthew. The song also functions on another level—as many gospel songs do—with the references to work and weariness, which indicate that the song likely has its origins in a work song sung by slaves. Like other spirituals, this one provides a rhythmic call and response that mimics the rhythm of work in the fields, even as its lyrics carry the workers outside of themselves in the expectation and hope of a new world where such work will be no more.

REFLECTION

"Keep Your Lamps Trimmed and Burning" delivers a timely message, but the song is not found in many hymnals these days. In fact, you're more likely to hear the song performed at a roots music concert than in a church. There may be several reasons for this omission by churches and for the song's embrace by the roots music community. One is certainly that the song is most often associated with blues musicians. Although many spirituals and gospel songs have their origin in the blues, many religious hearers reject association with music they think of as being "too worldly." Those listeners may want their music purified and stately rather than gritty and earthy. Another reason may be that it is simply too difficult for congregations to sing a song that has a call-and-response musical structure. Sometimes choirs will sing a version of this song as an anthem in a Sunday morning service, but sometimes those versions are sanitized and don't capture the spiraling, sing-song rhythm of the field chant and blues structure. Finally, the song focuses on the world to come and urges its listeners not to get weary in their work or in praying or preaching, because another, better world is coming soon. As one version puts it, the journey to heaven is "almost over." Very few churches in the early part of the twenty-first century look to the world to come and center their preaching or their work on the apocalypse, or the return of Jesus to come, and the preparations that individuals and the larger community must make to be ready for this change.

Even though "Keep Your Lamps Trimmed and Burning" is absent from the songbooks of many Christian communities, the song can still have an impact on our lives. Sometimes the music of a song—

apart from the lyrics—can move us powerfully, which is the case with "Keep Your Lamps Trimmed and Burning." The guitars and voices of every version, from Reverend Gary Davis's to the Tedeschi Trucks Band's, spiral higher and higher until reaching a climactic moment when the song becomes more urgent, before spiraling down to its last notes. The music is uplifting and transformative and redemptive, and if you enter the music itself as you listen, you will often find yourself moved and transformed. The dynamic energy of the music propels the lyrics and urges us to repeat them as we sing along with whatever version to which we might be listening. The lyrics become a kind of litany for us as the message of the song takes us out of ourselves and comforts us in the knowledge that God is ultimately in control of the world.

"Keep Your Lamps Trimmed and Burning" keeps us looking forward to a world where we'll no longer be bone-tired from oppression and weary of all the suffering that infuses our being. If we keep on working, preaching, and praying, we can prepare ourselves and help bring into being this new world where weariness and suffering are no more. We must not wait for others to perform these tasks of love and service for us—we cannot be like the foolish maids, in other words—but we must embrace those tasks ourselves and keep our lamps always filled with oil as we anticipate the advent of a more beautiful and just world: one that we help, with God's grace, shape.

EIGHT
HOW GREAT THOU ART

BACKGROUND

My FATHER WASN'T AN ESPECIALLY RELIGIOUS MAN. When I was in kindergarten and elementary school, he would drop my mother, my sister, and me off at church and pick us up after the service was finished. I have no idea how he spent those two or so hours every Sunday morning, and I surely didn't wonder why he wasn't coming in with us, for it wasn't all that unusual to see other fathers doing the same with their families.

When I was a teenager, I joined a youth group at the local Presbyterian church—because many of my friends were in the group, of course, and not because I recall being especially religious myself then—and I attended church there every Sunday morning. My mother and sister often attended the Baptist church across the street, but my father never attended either. I know he grew up attending church, for his parents were devout Methodists—at least his mother was—in a small South Carolina town. I also learned as I grew older that he had been very active in the ministry—he was a deacon and served on the finance committee—of the First Baptist Church in West Palm Beach, Florida. Still, it wasn't until I went to college, during which time my father lost his job, that I watched my father become more involved in our local Baptist church in Atlanta. Even then—he was deacon and an usher and a secretary in his Sunday school class—I couldn't tell how deep his faith went, for we never talked much about it, and he didn't seem to be very much changed by his religious experiences. Several years later, there was conflict in the church, and the church split; my father followed the beloved pastor he had come to admire to another church, but he eventually stopped going to church again—largely, I think, because of his health and the distance from our house to the church.

Even though my father had this ambivalent relationship with the church, he loved religious music, and it moved him so much that he would watch over and over videotapes of Bill Gaither concerts. (Gaither and his wife, Gloria, and other members of their family, were legendary gospel and contemporary Christian musicians.) Every Sunday morning, my dad would set the radios in the house to WPCH and listen to their programs of hymns and sacred music as he ate breakfast and then got ready to head off to Sunday school. He would continue to listen to the same station in the car on his way to the church. Many of the songs on that program were schmaltzy—at least in my opinion at the time—instrumental versions of familiar hymns, such as "O for a Thousand Tongues to Sing," "Come, Thou Almighty King," "Softly and Tenderly (Jesus Is Calling)," and "Amazing Grace," among many others, but also choirs singing "Rock of Ages," or "For the Beauty of the Earth," or "How Great Thou Art."

"How Great Thou Art" was very likely my father's favorite hymn. He first heard the song performed, as did many hundreds of others, by George Beverly Shea in the late 1950s during a televised performance of one of evangelist Billy Graham's crusades. Like others, my father—and my grandmother, who also loved both Graham and Shea, and who would sing along with Shea when she watched the revivals on television—was moved by Shea's powerful bass-baritone vocals. Before Billy Graham invited him to join the Billy Graham Evangelistic Association in 1950, Shea had already released at least one album of inspirational songs—including, among others, "If You Know the Lord" and "Tenderly He Watches"—at RCA, but once he joined Graham's organization, his career blossomed on the strength of singing the one song for which he became famous: "How Great Thou Art." Shea discovered the song almost by accident; on a trip to London to perform at a crusade, a publisher gave him the sheet music for the song after they happened to meet by chance on a London street. After his return home, Shea discovered the sheets, sang the song to himself, and liked it. He performed it first in Toronto, at a crusade in 1955, and the song became synonymous with Shea for decades.

"How Great Thou Art" originated in Sweden, where the Reverend Carl Boberg wrote a poem about the tempestuousness of a sudden storm over a local lake and the just as sudden return of peaceful calm after the storm passed. The thunder, wind, and lightning, according to Boberg's story, whipped up waves on the lake, but once the storm subsided, a rainbow appeared. Boberg wrote "*O Store Gud*" (O Great God) in response to his experience. Boberg's song passed through numerous translations—first into German, then into Russian, and then into English. A missionary couple to Russia, Mr. and Mrs. Stuart K. Hine, translated three verses and later added a fourth, and that is the form in which Shea received it and thus popularized it. It is also the song that is found in many hymnals today.

"HOW GREAT THOU ART"

"How Great Thou Art" offers a glorious meditation in song on the wonders of the natural world and God's glorious acts of creation, as well as a reflection on the overwhelming immensity of God's work in every area of our lives. The song also alludes to Psalm 8, a creation psalm, and the language of the song is very similar to the language of the psalm.

The familiar chorus begins, "Then sings my soul, / my Savior God, to thee," and the psalm begins, "O LORD, our Lord, how majestic is thy name in all the earth!" (Ps. 8:1) "How Great Thou Art" issues an acclamation to the glory of God, the glory of creation, and the role of humankind within the natural created order. Humankind's smallness in the face of the enormity of God and God's recognition of humankind is a theme that flows through the song, and in Psalm 8, the poet also feels his own smallness: "What is man that thou art mindful of him, and the son of man that thou dost care for him?" (Ps. 8:4).

Theologically, the structure of the song rehearses the history of human salvation. God creates. God provides and sustains. Humankind corrupts God's good creation, but in God's infinite wisdom and love, God sends his Son, "not sparing . . . him to die." The final verse of the song sings of the new creation that brings the salvation history full circle, from creation to restoration and new beginnings.

"How Great Thou Art" builds musically out from the chorus that sings praises to the greatness of God and God's creating and redeeming acts, and then the verses build layer by layer as they reach the climax of God's glorious new creation. Each verse—or stanza, since "How Great Thou Art" was originally a poem—has an ABAB rhyme scheme so that the endings of the first and third lines rhyme, and the endings of the second and fourth lines rhyme. The beauty of the rhyme lies in its inexactitude; some of the lines do rhyme naturally, but others are eye-rhymes—such as *wander* and *grandeur* in the second and fourth lines of the second verse.

The first verse of the song sets up the rest of the song. The speaker narrates this song from the perspective of wonder and awe at the way God's mighty power is displayed throughout the universe. In fact, the first two verses depict a natural theology in which God reveals God's self to the writer through nature. In the first verse, the writer recognizes the power of God by looking at the stars and hearing the rolling thunder; as in many biblical accounts, humans encounter God through sight and sound, and thunderstorms are often depicted as especially epiphanic moments in the Bible. Notice also in the first verse that God makes the world like a potter makes a pot, with his hands; "God's hands" make the "worlds" the writer sees around him. For us, hearing the song today, the word *worlds* has a far different meaning than it might have when the writer composed this poem, for the word now reminds us that God created the worlds that intersect with our human world, not only those we can see in the sky, but all of the ecological webs in which we find ourselves woven. Thus, the first verse not only jubilantly celebrates the displays of God's creative power, but it also contemplates breathlessly the awesome majesty of God's power, staring almost speechlessly at the stars and listening intently to the thunder.

The second verse of the song intensifies the first verse, listing all the wonders of nature that the writer sees or hears or feels. This is the verse that the Hines added to the song, and it underscores God's revelatory activity within the natural world. When God discloses God's self to us in nature, God is preparing us for a fuller revelation of God in Jesus. Even so, when God's revelations come through nature, we know and see the beauty of the world around us, our relation to others in it, and the awesome majesty of the created order. In this second verse, the writer "wanders" through "woods and forest glades"; he hears the birds "sing sweetly in the trees"; he looks "down from lofty mountain grandeur"; and he hears "the brook, and feel[s] the gentle breeze." The gentle images of the living beauty, the purity, and grandness of the world lead his soul to sing to his Savior God: "How great thou art! How great thou art!"

The third verse of "How Great Thou Art" moves from God's activity in the natural world to God's activity in the human world. The third verse moves from natural theology in which we respond faithfully to God's revelation of God's self in nature, to an incarnational theology in which we respond faithfully to God's revealing God's self to us in Jesus. Moreover, God sends his Son, Jesus, who dies on the Cross for our sins, according to the song and to the traditional theological view of God's sacrifice for humanity. The verse shifts from images involving the senses— smelling, seeing, feeling—to an image involving reason and reflection: "when I think." Having been led into God's presence by the majesty and wonder of nature, the writer is now led into the mysterious transaction that involves God's redeeming us by the sacrifice of God's Son. The writer—and we by extension—can "scarce take it in," so wondrous is God's activity on our behalf. Just as the forests and the birds' songs lead us to sing God's praises, so God's redemptive activity leads us to sing: "How great thou art!"

In the fourth verse, we experience God's final revelation: we see God face-to-face and "bow in humble adoration." With natural revelation, we see God's power in nature, and God prepares our hearts to receive his presence. If we have only natural revelation, however, we can never know God fully, so we only know God in a limited way. When God reveals God's self to us in Christ, we are prepared through natural revelation to receive this new and more complete knowledge. We begin to see God more fully and can sing God's praises even louder since we now see more facets of God. We know God most fully when we meet God face-to-face; this is the final revelation, and the final verse of "How Great Thou Art" celebrates the power and wonder of this revelation. "Christ [comes] with shouts of acclamation" and takes us "home." Joy fills our hearts when this happens, and our response is to "bow in humble adoration" before God. Once again, but this time more loudly, we proclaim, "My God, how great thou art!"

REFLECTION

In November 2016, country artists Vince Gill and Carrie Underwood delivered a stunning performance of "How Great Thou Art" at the legendary Ryman Auditorium in Nashville, Tennessee. In her soaring vocals, Underwood captured the song's praise and adoration of the world's beauty as it reflects God's majesty. Underwood wiped away tears as she finished her performance, a sign of how deeply the song embedded itself in her heart and soul.

Hearing and singing this song affects many people the same way. This is another tune whose musical setting is so majestic that it moves us, even without our hearing the lyrics. Since "How Great Thou Art" was one of my father's favorite songs, we asked Glen Sloan, the extraordinary pianist at John's Creek Baptist Church in Alpharetta, Georgia, to play the hymn as part of his prelude music for my father's memorial service. Even though we were not singing the words, the music touched us deeply.

"How Great Thou Art" often appears in hymnals in sections titled "Glory to the Triune God," and such a description captures the major theme of the song. During our worship services, we sing the song to glorify God's greatness, to recall God's role as Creator and sustainer of us and our world, and to praise the beauty of the world around us. In those moments when we are singing "How Great Thus Art," we are ascending higher and higher in our knowledge and in our adoration of God, just as we are embracing the worlds that surround us in that moment and in our lives outside of worship.

When we enter our communities singing "How Great Thou Art," we acknowledge that God is worthy of our adoration and that we can approach our God humbly and on bended knee. Singing the song is an act of worship—the worship of God in the natural created order, the worship of God's love and providence, and the worship of the God who is working with us to restore a more just and loving order. We can worship the God who reveals God's self through nature, Christ, and a restored creation by giving ourselves over to the music and allowing the swelling sounds to wash over us as we allow the lyrics to echo through our souls. In that moment, "How Great Thou Art" transforms us—even as it can transform communities—and it transports us out of ourselves into a restored relationship with our Creator.

There are close to two thousand recorded versions of "How Great Thou Art," ranging from Shea's, Underwood's, and Elvis Presley's to those by country singers Alan Jackson and Dolly Parton, as well as those by Christian artists Amy Grant and the Blackwood Brothers Quartet. Listen to any version of "How Great Thou Art" and reflect on the greatness of God, on the loving activity of God as Creator, and on the beauty of our world. Think about how God works in the world today. Reflect on the meaning of the words "bow in humble adoration"; what do we adore today? Does anyone—do even religious people—value and practice humility these days? Are we prepared to bow before God in humility to adore him? How do our worship services lead us to practice "humble adoration"? What worship practices lead us to practice acts of adoration during the worship service? In what measure can singing "How Great Thou Art" transport us beyond ourselves toward a different, or new, relationship with God? How can singing "How Great Thou Art" help us reshape our relationship to nature? "How Great Thou Art" changes us and redirects our vision about our world and God.

NINE

WHEN GOD DIPS HIS PEN OF LOVE IN MY HEART

BACKGROUND

OSPEL MUSIC COMES IN MANY FORMS, and bluegrass gospel is one of the most popular forms of gospel music. The combination of mandolin, fiddle, bass, guitar, banjo, and sometimes vocals carries traditional gospel songs such as "I Saw the Light," "I'll Fly Away," "Farther Along," and "Will the Circle Be Unbroken?" in a scampering musical flight to bright and sprightly spheres.

Bill Monroe, Ricky Skaggs, Brooke Justice Aldridge and Darin Aldridge, and many others consider gospel music a key part of bluegrass, and they close (or closed) every set they play with a gospel song or two, often inviting the audience to sing along with them. Though "When God Dips His Pen of Love in My Heart" had its origins in the historically black church in the United States, one of the most popular versions of the song is by the bluegrass singers Alison Krauss and the Cox Family, who is well known in Christian music circles.

"When God Dips His Pen of Love in My Heart," however, is not a song we sing much in church these days. It's not in many hymnals, either, and in many ways its musical structure doesn't lend it to congregational singing. It's possible that many Christians are unfamiliar with the song—unless they're fans of Hank Williams or Alison Krauss and the Cox Family or any number of other country singers such as Red Foley, Jim Reeves, or Connie Smith. But it's a gospel song that stands with many more familiar songs as a musical expression of God's love and grace.

Although the Blackwood Brothers gospel quartet recorded one the earliest versions of the song, it was written by Reverend Cleavant Derricks, a Tennessee native who became a pastor and choir director in several different churches from the Washington, DC, area to Dallas, Texas, where he spent most of his time leading congregations and writing songs. He sold many of his songs to Stamps-Baxter Publishing, which then gave them to many popular artists to record. In addition to "When God Dips His Pen of Love in My Heart," Derricks wrote "Just a Little Talk with Jesus," "When He Blessed My Soul," and "We'll Soon Be Done with Troubles and Trials," most of which transmitted inspirational messages to his congregations during the difficult years of the Great Depression. Jerry Lee Lewis and Elvis Presley recorded a duet of "Just a Little Talk with Jesus" in 1956, and Tennessee Ernie Ford also recoded a version of the song.

"WHEN GOD DIPS HIS PEN OF LOVE IN MY HEART"

A FEW YEARS AGO, COUNTRY SINGER JESSICA STILES released her version of "When God Dips His Pen of Love in My Heart." It's a bright shuffle that captures the joy that the song's lyrics proclaim. Stiles evokes the spirit of the song so well because she punctuates the refrain with "Hallelujahs," exclamations of the praise she raises to God for God's love, the ways God has made her whole, and her gratitude for God's rich blessings, especially for God's gift of salvation. Alison Krauss and the Cox Family's version mimics Cleavant Derricks's original, opening with the singers humming in harmony and then launching into a blues-inflected, high, lonesome sound underscored by a haunting banjo and guitar riffs. The musical spaciousness of Krauss and the Cox Family's version blossoms into a jubilant celebration of God's love. The heavenly vocals of Krauss and the Cox Family create an ethereal sound that floats into our hearts and infects us with joy.

As with many gospel songs, the opening line of the first verse of "When God Dips His Pen of Love in My Heart" provides the song's title. This first verse depicts the actions of a loving God who claims us as God's beloved by an act we don't often associate with God: writing. There are several biblical images of God writing on our hearts; those images depict God delivering a new covenant, an interior covenant of love that fills us and directs us. In Jeremiah 31:33, the prophet delivers God's message that God will put his law within the people, and God "will write it upon their hearts." The writer of Hebrews 8:10 quotes Jeremiah 31:33, altering it a little but reiterating that God will put God's laws "into their minds, and write them on their hearts." "When God Dips His Pen of Love in My Heart" evokes this biblical imagery in the opening verse, scrolling out the consequences of God's scribbling in the following verses. Additionally, the song's opening line contains a startling image. Long ago when writers used quill pens or fountain pens, they would dip their pens into an ink well to replenish the ink in their pens so they could write more words. The action of dipping one's pen is very quick and doesn't interrupt the process of writing for long. Thus, God quickly dips God's pen into a heart that is murky, like ink, but in this case God doesn't draw out but writes and leaves words behind on the singer's heart.

The first line—"When God dips His pen of love in my heart"— is repeated as the final line of the verse to reiterate God's action of inscribing God's message of love on the singer's heart. The second line of the first verse reveals what God does when God dips God's pen: "He writes my soul a message He wants me to know." As a result, the singer's soul overflows with love because God's "spirit all divine fills this sinful soul of mine." If the singer's soul is an ink well into which God dips God's pen, then God not only writes a message of love and redemption on his heart but also draws out the darkness of his soul, filling it with light.

The song's chorus and refrain evoke the feeling of the singer whose soul brims over with joy. In the Gospel stories of Jesus's healings, Jesus often tells the person he's healed not to share the good news of the healing. This has puzzled Jesus-followers for centuries. The chorus of "When God Dips His Pen of Love in My Heart" builds and opens with an image based on these stories: "I said I wouldn't tell it to a living soul / How He brought salvation when He made me whole." The singer may be reluctant to tell any of his friends how deeply he has been changed by God's love; he also may feel reticent about telling others about the way in which God has imprinted God's message on his heart. Such a feeling is temporary, though, since the singer finds he "couldn't hide / Such love as Jesus did impart." Like the people Jesus healed, who simply can't keep quiet about their experience and must share it with their family and community, the singer can't contain his joy and must tell others. The refrain, which repeats the song's opening line, describes how the singer feels when God dips his pen in his heart: "It makes me laugh and it makes me cry / Sets my sinful soul on fire." God's generous message of love and grace moves the singer to joy and to tears. Overcome with these feelings, he can't help crying, not just because he recognizes his shortcomings ("my sinful soul"), but because he can't believe he's worthy of God's gracious actions. He laughs simply because this seems so absurd to him, but he also laughs with joy. Now that God has dipped his pen of love in his heart, he's a soul on fire—that is, he has a heart warmed by God's presence and love, and the singer now has a fiery passion to share God's love and grace with others.

In the second verse of "When God Dips His Pen of Love in My Heart," the singer acknowledges that God's generous gift of changing his heart doesn't mean that every day of life will be bright and without its trials. Life is filled with difficulties and challenges. Our daily journeys can be lonely walks on which we sometimes feel as if God has abandoned us. Sometimes our pain and sorrow are so overwhelming that we can't complete simple tasks and can't get through the daily work of life. Moreover, sometimes we experience such pain and sorrow that we fail to love the God who loves us, or we fail to share the goodness of God with others because we are so overcome by our own grief. Even though the burdens of this life sometimes weigh heavily on the singer—"Sometimes the way is dreary, dark, and cold / And some unburdened sorrow keeps me from the goal"—the singer knows that God is always there, written on his heart, and that when he prays to God, he can always listen to God's voice as it "whispers sweet peace to my soul." Like "What a Friend We Have in Jesus," "When God Dips His Pen of Love in My Heart" offers assurance that God remains close to us through every trial we experience, and we simply need to remember God's presence and that we can petition God in prayer.

The final verse of "When God Dips His Pen of Love in My Heart" reiterates that Jesus gave his life for us on the Cross so that we could be free of sin and we could live a "better day." These final lines underscore God's love for us, but they also describe the dramatic ways in which God cleanses the sin from our hearts and souls. Just as in the first verse the singer contrasts his sinful soul with the message of love that God writes on his heart, here the singer contrasts God's love and the singer's sin: "My life was steeped in sin but in love He took me in / His blood washed away every stain." The singer also contrasts the overwhelming love that God through Jesus has for us: "[He] gave His life completely to bring a better day." In contrast, because we allow ourselves to be overwhelmed by our sorrows and our shortcomings, we cannot give ourselves completely to God. Thankfully, according to the song, God walks every step of our rugged ways with us, dipping his pen of love in our hearts to write continually on our souls God's message of love and grace and redemption and hope.

REFLECTION

What would it mean to you for God to dip God's pen of love in your heart? How does this image of God's intimate love resonate with you? Have you ever had the experience of feeling as if God is physically touching you? How did you feel? How did you try to describe that experience to others? How did others respond when you tried to describe that experience? Were you, as the song says, moved to laugh and cry? How has your life changed by considering that God's love is written on your heart?

Listen to a few different versions of "When God Dips His Pen of Love in My Heart." What are the differences you hear between Cleavant Derricks's original version and Alison Krauss and the Cox Family's version? Where do you hear the joy in the song? Where do you hear sorrow? Choose one of these versions—or another of the many versions of the song—and reflect on just what it means for God to dip God's pen in your heart. Is this a comforting feeling? Does the promise of such activity on the part of God inspire you or make you tremble a little? Reflect on what it means to be marked by God with God's law of love written on your heart.

Reflect for a moment on the act of writing. Reflect for a moment on the power of the written word to endure. Meditate on the power of the written word to change lives.

"When God Dips His Pen of Love in My Heart" is one of those gospel songs that move us as much musically as they do lyrically. Whether it's Cleavant Derricks's barrelhouse piano flowing under the swelling choral harmonies of his singers or the jazzy bluegrass swing and heavenly vocals of Alison Krauss and the Cox Family, the music transports us out of ourselves and moves our hearts. Then, when we listen closely to the lyrics, we're moved in a different way to embrace God's deep love for us. For these reasons, "When God Dips His Pen of Love in My Heart" is a gospel song that can change your life.

Ten
STANDING ON
THE PROMISES

BACKGROUND

MANY OF THE GREATEST, OR MOST MEMORABLE, gospel songs came out of a crisis in the life of the author of the song. "Amazing Grace" grew out of John Newton's dramatic conversion experience. "Precious Lord, Take My Hand" conveys the depth of Thomas Dorsey's sorrow and grief. "What a Friend We Have in Jesus" grew out of Joseph M. Scriven's longing to comfort his mother when they were separated by a long distance. "Will the Circle Be Unbroken?"—especially the Carter Family version—came from A. P. Carter's mourning and sorrow. Even songs such as "Steal Away to Jesus" and "Swing Low, Sweet Chariot" were created out of an urgency and need to escape the unbearable conditions of the singers' world.

"Standing on the Promises" was written with an affirmation of the power and goodness of God during a time of searching for God's presence. The song's author, Russell Kelso Carter, was born into a strong Christian home, but as he grew older he struggled to make a commitment to God. When he was a teenager he became a Christian and started attending a Presbyterian church. Before he was twenty-five, Carter started having heart trouble and moved from his home in Pennsylvania to California, hoping that work as a rancher might improve his health. When it did not, he sought out a popular Boston minister named Charles Cullis, who conducted faith healings. Cullis prayed for Carter, and he was healed, and after this incident Carter sought to grow closer to God. In his early thirties, he wrote theological tracts about the miracle of healing, contending that Jesus died not just for our sins but also for our sicknesses. Carter wrote several songs that grew out of his experience of sickness and healing, interpreting them in light of his ideas about the power of Jesus to heal body and soul. Some of the songs he wrote include "Promises of a Perfect Love" and "Hymns of the Christian Life." His most famous song is "Standing on the Promises."

"STANDING ON THE PROMISES"

The Sensational Nightingales' version of "Standing on the Promises" opens slowly and blossoms into a call-and-response sermon that embraces the exalted promise that God's words and actions sustain us in whatever circumstances life brings our way. The gospel quartet shouts and preaches to the crowd midway through the song, bringing to life the words and delivering hope that when we claim God's promises for us—God's love, God's hope, God's mercy, God's justice—then we can live a fuller life dedicated to God, others, and the world. We must first embrace all that God offers us—"stand on the promises"—and then we can live a life blessed by God.

Standing on the promises, though, never comes easy, for we all experience moments of doubt about the faithfulness of God, about God's power to effect change in this world, about the very existence of a God who somehow relates to the world in which we live. Yet this "Standing on the Promises" arises out of the experience of faithfulness to the God who made many promises to God's people in the Bible—the promise of deliverance from captivity, the promise always to go with God's people, the promise to protect God's people in every situation, the promise to raise up a king who would watch over God's people, the promise to establish a new covenant with God's people, the promise to deliver a Savior to God's people. The song affirms God's faithfulness and claims that human faithfulness to God's promises is a response to God's faithfulness to humans.

What does it mean to "stand on the promises of God"? The language of this song is a bit archaic, for we seldom, even in churches, utter this phrase—although there are several Christian traditions, such as the Baptist and the Pentecostal churches, that still use this phrase. Even though the author of the hymn penned it when he was a practicing Methodist, United Methodists very seldom sing the song, despite its being collected in their hymnbooks.

Why would we sing about "standing on the promises of God"? Literally, of course, to stand on the promises of God is to put our feet solidly on the ground of our faith. If we are standing on the promises of God, we're standing upon a solid platform of faith from which we can tell others about our faith. The platform of God's promises is solid, and we're assured of its strength and security. Another common way of describing "standing on the promises" is by saying that we "claim the promises of God." This language can also sound archaic, but it operates on a very simple premise: if anyone makes a promise to us, we can claim that gift for ourselves—for a promise involves a gift of trust—knowing that the gift cannot be taken away. Sadly, friends and family break promises many times, so we often have difficulty claiming those promises when they are given to us. God, though, never breaks promises, and the biblical stories of God's promises assure us we can claim these promises and rest assured that God's promises of love and grace will never be broken. Claiming God's promises binds us more strongly to God and helps us to endure as we struggle daily with fear, anxiety, loss, despair, uncertainty, or doubt.

Unlike some other spirituals or gospel songs, "Standing on the Promises" does not open with a refrain. The song opens with a verse that does supply the key terms for the refrain that follows the opening verse—and is repeated following each verse—so the key theme of the song is announced right away. Moreover, the song maintains its lyrical structure by repeating the first line of the first verse as the opening line of each subsequent verse, altering only slightly the last few words of each line. In the first verse, the singers proclaim that they're "standing on the promises of Christ my King," and the language of the remainder of this verse focuses on the activity of adoring and praising a king who provides for his people. The singers let their "praises ring," they adore their Christ the king by giving him "glory in the highest," and they "shout and sing." The first verse also proclaims that the singers will let their praises of the Christ, who has promised to be their king and bring in a new kingdom—a promise derived from the biblical stories of Jesus in the Gospels and Jesus's ushering in the kingdom of God—ring through the "eternal ages." According to this song and according to the stories of the Gospels, Christ promises to be with us always, even until the "close of the age" (Matt. 28:20). When we stand on, or claim, this promise of God, we too can rest assured that God accompanies us always in this life, even until we die, and we can praise and shout and sing to the glory of God's eternal goodness and sustenance.

The second verse of "Standing on the Promises" claims the power of the promises of God to sustain individuals as they experience the "howling storms of doubt and fear." The singers affirm in the first line of the verse that they're "standing on the promises that cannot fail." We can be confident, according to these lyrics, in God's promises because—as recorded in the Bible—they never falter, so we can put our trust in them. This verse bolsters our confidence that the "living Word of God"—which is a description of Jesus and thus parallel to the title "Christ my King" in the first verse—prevails over the stormy periods in our lives, including the loss of a job, death of a loved one, death of a child, death of a relationship, bankruptcy, and eviction. In the Gospels, Jesus prevails over his own darkness as he renounces the Tempter. If we claim the promise that Jesus will stand with us when we face the same kinds of dark days, we can overcome the fears and the storms in our lives. Just when the clouds grow darkest, the song tells us, the living Word of God is our closest companion, helping us endure through these gloomy and anxious times. The refrain follows this verse as a reminder that we are constantly "standing, standing / Standing on the promises of God."

Although the power of darkness is strong and can defeat us if we allow it to do so, the power of love is even greater, and it pushes out the darkness from our lives. The third verse of

"Standing on the Promises" focuses on God's promise to bind us to God with love, as well as to provide us with a spiritual aid in overcoming difficulties in our daily lives. The first line of the verse offers yet another description of Jesus—"Christ the Lord"—as a parallel to "Christ the King" and the "living Word of God" in the previous two verses. Here, the promise of God we can claim is to be "bound to him [Christ the Lord] eternally by love's strong cord." We never need to fear, because we are so tightly bound to God's love for us through the incarnate God, Christ. Once we claim the promise that we are inextricably bound to Christ by love, we can then claim, also, the promise of an aid who supports, fortifies, and bolsters us as we face daily challenges or doubts about our faith. In addition to being bound by the strong cord of love, we can overcome our challenges "daily with the Spirit's sword." The imagery in these two lines is striking: one is an image of domesticity—love—while the other is a martial image—the sword. What's also striking about these two lines is that the "sword" can sever bonds or a "cord." In the song, however, the "Spirit's sword" may be a reference to the Bible (often referred to as the sword of the Lord). Our claim of the promise—the promise that with the Spirit's sword we can overcome daily—may well refer to the ways that daily Bible study empowers us to deal with challenging situations. This verse exhorts us to claim the promise of God's love and the Spirit's help as we try to overcome doubts about our faith, or as we face anxiously the challenges of daily life.

The fourth and final verse of "Standing on the Promises" brings the song full circle, closing with an affirmation that if we claim the promises of God, we "cannot fail." The final verse links together three gerunds—*standing, listening, resting*—that describe the ways we claim the promises of God. Because we are bound tightly by love to Christ, and because the Holy Spirit is our advocate in overcoming our daily challenges, when we're "standing on the promises," we "cannot fail." Moreover, our faithful listening to the voice of the Spirit—"listening every moment to the Spirit's call"—as well as to the words of Jesus in the Bible directs us to love others and to claim the promises that allow us to weather the storminess of life. Finally, when we can confidently rest in the love of Jesus—"resting in my Savior as my all in all"—we can claim the peace, mercy, love, and grace that God shares with us through Jesus and the Holy Spirit. When we are standing, listening, and resting, we cannot fail. The refrain following this final verse both serves as a reminder that we can and should claim the promises of God and also delivers exalted praise to God for God's promises with joy that we can claim them.

REFLECTION

Where are the places in your life that you experience darkness? In times when you have experienced loss—the loss of a job, the loss of a loved one through death, the loss of a relationship, the loss of your faith, the loss of financial stability—how have you dealt with the gloom and despair of those losses? Have these times of darkness and loss driven you to despair and doubt? Has your faith helped you though these crises, or have they caused you to doubt your faith and God's power to help you weather them?

Listen to several versions of "Standing on the Promises." The Sensational Nightingales' version and Alan Jackson's version offer two distinct approaches to the gospel song, so you may want to listen to these two versions so you can hear the differences that each musician gives to different parts of the song. As you listen to various versions of "Standing on the Promises," imagine that you are standing on a pier in the middle of a body of water; the water roils turbulently around you, and sometimes you feel the pier shake with the violent motion of the waves, but you are safe in the midst of the storm.

As you let the words and music wash over you, think of the promises of God as the pier, and the roiling waters as the storms that lap at your life every day. Reflect on God's promises to humans—whether these are promises you have learned about in a religious community or through your reading of the Bible—and ask yourself how they can comfort you. Are these promises solid, like the pier on which you're standing in your imagination? If you haven't claimed these promises, do you want to claim them? How can you claim them?

"Standing on the Promises" provides a glimpse of the ways that we can embrace God's many promises. The repetitious refrain builds layer by layer into a joyous affirmation that God is with us always, sustaining us with love, grace, mercy, and hope. For these reasons, is there any doubt that "Standing on the Promises" is a gospel song that can change your life?

Eleven

IF HEAVEN NEVER WAS PROMISED TO ME

BACKGROUND

URING THE SUMMER between my junior and senior year in college, I played in a Jesus band—the popular name then for a band that blended the rhythms of rock and roll with the message of the Gospels. (You should have seen my hair back then!) This was in the summer of 1975, so there were numerous musicians who were already trying to make the message of Jesus relevant to youth who were questioning the relevance of religion and the church. Many were also searching to find spiritual meaning in their lives.

The gates had already opened in 1970 with the rock opera *Jesus Christ Superstar*, and again in 1971 with the musical *Godspell*. Each of these musical-theater productions featured crowds of young people yearning to find meaning in their lives, and searching to discover how the church, in particular, and Christianity, in general, could provide such meaning in their lives. After all, the church preached love and acceptance, didn't it? Yet many long-haired, "freaky" people didn't feel accepted when they walked through church doors. More often than not, young men and women with long hair, wearing tattered jeans or flowery skirts, carrying torn backpacks with all their belongings in them, were turned away at the church doors.

The final verse of a popular song, "Signs," by the Five Man Electrical Band, expresses both the alienation and the hope that a young man feels when he walks into a traditional church setting: "The sign said, everyone welcome, come in kneel down and pray / But when they passed around the plate at the end of it all / I didn't have a penny to pay." The young man takes out a pen and some paper and writes a note thanking the Lord for thinking about him since, he sings, he's "alive and doing fine."

Every Friday night, the band I played in would gather on the stage of the Chapel by the Lake, an outdoor worship venue built and owned by the First Baptist Church of West Palm Beach, Florida. The then-pastor Jess Moody had a vision in the early 1960s of an outdoor chapel, situated across the street from the church and backing up to Lake Worth. Moody and other pastors preached from a pulpit designed as a ship's prow; musicians, choirs, and bands would fill the risers behind the pulpit. On those summer Friday nights in 1975, Teens Alive for God rallies were held in the Chapel by the Lake. High school and college students—some already involved in local churches, but many others not involved in any churches—flocked to the event, which featured evangelistic preaching, baptisms, and music. Our band, the Teens Alive for God band, played songs by contemporary Christian music artists, including Larry Norman, Ken Medema, Kurt Kaiser—whose song "Pass It On" functioned as a benediction for many of our meetings—as well as songs from Christian rock musicals such as *Show Me!* by Jimmy and Carol Owens and *Jesus Christ Superstar* and *Godspell*. We also played several songs by Andraé Crouch, an artist and writer who combined the call-and-response structure of traditional gospel music with strains of soul, jazz, and blues in songs such as "My Tribute (To God Be the Glory)," "Soon and Very Soon," "Jesus Is the Answer," and "If Heaven Never Was Promised to Me."

Even though I played in the Jesus band, I was struggling with my own Christian identity. I was also playing in a few rock bands at the time, and I certainly embraced the lifestyle of a rock musician, even though I was raised in a Christian family, attended church every Sunday, and became a Christian as a teenager. Still, by the time I was sitting under the stars on those summer Friday nights, I wasn't sure whether I could easily embrace the message to which I was testifying through my music. But one night, as I was sitting there on stage between songs, my mind wandering as the preacher exclaimed the Good News of Jesus to the gathered crowd, a moment of peace washed over me as I felt a unity with God, nature, and the others attending the service. Only a few moments earlier, we had played Crouch's song "If Heaven Never Was Promised to Me," and while I had been playing it every night and searching for guitar parts that would give the song a fresh sound, I listened closely to the words that night. When we sang the lines of the chorus—"If heaven never was promised to me . . . / It's been worth just having the Lord in my life"—I realized that being a Christian didn't mean simply living in order to get into heaven and stay out of hell, which was the Christianity with which I had been raised.

Crouch's song taught me that living the Christian life meant experiencing God's powerful love here in this world, in this time and space, and sharing God's love with others by loving them through my words and actions. Crouch's song liberated me—though I probably wouldn't have described it this way at the time—for after that night I started to participate in prison ministry, playing guitar and leading the singing in services at a local minimum-security prison and accompanying a local preacher on trips to a maximum-security prison in south central Florida. When I was invited to play in churches in the area, I played "If Heaven Never Was Promised to Me" because the song conveys such a powerful message about living one's Christian life in the messiness of the world.

BACKGROUND

When Andraé Crouch died in January 2015, he left a musical legacy that reached deeply, not only into gospel music but also into popular music. Crouch conducted the choirs that sang in Michael Jackson's hit song "Man in the Mirror" and in Madonna's hit song "Like a Prayer," and he wrote and arranged the music for the television series *Amen*. His songs appeared in movies from *The Color Purple* ("Heaven Belongs to You" and "God Is Trying to Tell You Something") and *Borat* ("The Blood Will Never Lose Its Power") to *Downsizing* ("My Tribute [To God Be the Glory]") and *Marjoe* ("I've Got Confidence"). Crouch won six GMA (Gospel Music Association) Dove Awards and seven Grammys, either for his work as a solo artist or for his work with Andraé Crouch and the Disciples. Above all, Crouch's greatest and most enduring achievement remains his ability to combine gospel and rock in such a way that churches began to incorporate new sounds into their congregational singing and into their hymnals.

Crouch also brought the rhythms of jazz and soul into gospel music, so deeply transforming gospel music that listeners outside of churches embraced it and were moved by its acclamations and shouts of joy.

Andraé Crouch's musical genius emerged early in his life. When he was eleven, Crouch's father became the interim pastor at a local church, and one Sunday the congregation encouraged the young Crouch to play piano for the service. Soon after, he was writing his own music, composing his first song, "The Blood Will Never Lose Its Power," when he was fourteen. By 1960, when he was eighteen, he had formed his first gospel group, the Church of God in Christ Singers, which included the great rock and soul keyboard player Billy Preston. Crouch also formed a gospel group, The Disciples, in 1965, and he soon signed a publishing agreement with Manna Music Publishing for his first song, "The Blood Will Never Lose Its Power." By 1968, Andraé Crouch and The Disciples had a recording contract with Light Records, releasing their first album, *Take the Message Everywhere*, which was recorded by the famous Christian music producer Ralph Carmichael. During the 1970s and 1980s, Crouch, either with The Disciples or in his solo career, deeply influenced the direction of gospel music, Jesus rock, and what soon came to be known as contemporary Christian music.

Above all else, Andraé Crouch was a fearless innovator, ceaselessly inventive, always looking for ways to improve gospel music, including incorporating secular music into gospel music. When he formed The Disciples in the mid-1960s, he included black and white singers and musicians, an innovation that at the time only the rock group Sly and the Family Stone had dared. The concerts of Andraé Crouch and The Disciples in churches, at revivals, and later in large arenas and concert halls brought a new sound to the Jesus music of the time. Instead of the folk, rock-tinged music of Larry Norman and Ken Medema, Crouch's gospel songs exploded with a rhythmic beat whose energy grew more propulsive with every verse, carrying its listeners higher and higher toward a moment of transformation or renewal or joy in the Christian life. Crouch's gospel music is all about joy, and the topics he covers in his songs range from certainty in one's faith—"Jesus Is the Answer"—to praise for God's goodness—"My Tribute (To God Be the Glory)"—to the joyfulness of music and the power of faith—"I'm Gonna Keep on Singin'"—to the hope that Jesus will return—"Soon and Very Soon"—to faith's capacity to see us through our darkest moments—"I've Got Confidence." His songs rejoice mightily in the affirmation that Jesus brings the joy of salvation to a world living in darkness. Among Crouch's most enduring and transforming songs is "If Heaven Never Was Promised to Me," which he recorded on an album called *Just Andraé*.

"IF HEAVEN NEVER WAS PROMISED TO ME"

"If Heaven Never Was Promised to Me" opens quietly and sparely with Crouch weaving single notes into rolling chords on his piano. The sonic spaciousness of the song's opening invites listeners into the quiet beauty of the music as they consider the song's lyrics. The song allows us to breathe and relax into a moment of reflection on our faith and on our theological journey.

In the first verse, Crouch's vocals play call and response with the notes he plays on the piano, creating an atmosphere that welcomes meditation on timeless questions: Why should I serve the Lord? Why am I a Christian? What is the relationship between my faith and the world in which I live? Am I Christian because God has promised me an eternal life in heaven where the streets are paved with gold and my thirst is always quenched?

In an elegant and simple melody, Crouch's baritone vocals weave around and under the simple piano notes, and he articulates these questions in a simple statement: "You may ask me why I serve the Lord." In the first two verses of the song, Crouch offers a litany of standard responses to such questions. People might serve the Lord "for heaven's gain," "to walk those mighty streets of gold," "to hear the angels sing," to "drink from the fountain / That never shall run dry," to "live forever . . . in that sweet, sweet by and by." During these verses, a lead guitar weaves notes around Crouch's vocals and his piano chords. At the end of the second verse, a flute evokes the ethereal character of the "sweet by and by."

The music builds layer by layer through the song, adding harmony vocals that emphasize the urgency of Crouch's message. By the time the song reaches its first chorus, we've started climbing to a higher ground on which Crouch declares that all these promises of heaven aren't reason enough for serving the Lord. In that chorus, Crouch offers the real reason for serving the Lord: "But if heaven never was promised to me / Neither God's presence to live eternally / It's been worth just having the Lord in my life / Living in a world of darkness / You came along and brought me the light." As the music builds to its climactic moments, the singers affirm over and over that the reason for serving God lies not in hoping that living for God will result in an afterlife in a resplendent heaven; instead, the value of serving the Lord is in bringing light to a world of darkness, just as Christ brought light to a world of darkness. By the time the song reaches the final verse, the singer can affirm the essence of the Christian life and embrace it: "If there were never any streets of gold / Neither a land where we'll never grow old / It's been worth just having the Lord in my life / You've been my closest friend down through the years / And every time I cry You dry my tears." Crouch ingeniously juxtaposes the promised beauty of an otherworldly realm with the simplicity and directness of friendship and love; we follow God—who stands with us in our darkest hours as a good friend would—because God loves us, not because God rewards us. Our reward is living out God's love in our worlds of darkness and bringing light to others.

REFLECTION

What does it mean to live the Christian life? Do we serve God because we've been promised rewards in an afterlife—rewards that keep us looking past the world around us to sweeter, more beautiful, less ugly, and less messy world beyond? Does God really promise us that if we serve the Lord faithfully, then we'll be rewarded with a new life in heaven where streets are paved with gold? How do we serve the Lord in this life if we continue to look beyond it to another life?

What if, as Crouch asks, "heaven never was promised to" us? If we could live into this question, how would we live our Christian lives differently? If "heaven never was promised to" us, could we affirm that it's been worth just having the Lord in our lives?

When Crouch released this song in 1973, many people were searching for a way of expressing their faith that they found more meaningful than the Christianity with which many of them had been raised. (I should know. I was there. I was one of them.) It was a time when many churches turned away from confronting social questions of the time—racism, inequality, and militarism, especially—and urged looking to the promise of an afterlife as a reward for affirming the teachings of the church and avoiding personal sinfulness and embracing personal salvation. When individuals proclaimed that they knew Jesus as their personal Savior, that proclamation very often meant that people were focusing on themselves, reassuring themselves that as long as they strove for holiness, they would be justly rewarded. They often seemed never to consider the world outside of themselves and their church: as long as they attended Sunday school, prayer meeting, and church faithfully, they were adding up heavenly rewards. Moreover, when Jesus returned to earth in cataclysmic fashion, he would embrace them as his own, taking them with him to heaven since they were faithful Christians. This way of thinking is still prevalent today. The questions this song poses are with us today as well—they've surely been faced by believers of every generation. "If Heaven Never Was Promised to Me" remains relevant as Christians continue to confront how to live a meaningful Christian life.

Crouch's song challenges us to look beyond ourselves, to turn away from looking toward a heavenly reward for our earthly actions, and to ask hard questions about the nature of our faith. "If Heaven Never Was Promised to Me" encourages us to question our faith; it encourages us to consider the shape of a meaningful Christian faith. Crouch's song can change our lives by inspiring us to consider what it means to live the Christian life as if heaven didn't exist; how would we live our Christian lives differently? The song opens new possibilities for living the Christian life. The closeness we experience with God—"You've been my closest friend down through the years"— especially as we experience pain, moves us to share that closeness with others by helping them dry their tears and by comforting them in their pain. As the song points out, we live in a world of darkness, and God brings light to that world; as God brings light into our own darkness, we are compelled to bring God's light into the darkness of the worlds in which others live. "If Heaven Never Was Promised to Me," therefore, is a gospel song that can change our lives.

TWELVE
I'LL FLY AWAY

BACKGROUND

"I'LL FLY AWAY" may be one of the few gospel songs sampled or recorded by rap artists. On his debut album, *College Dropout*, Kanye West delivers a stunningly beautiful performance of this one. With gorgeous harmonies floating over a spare piano arrangement, West and his backup singers sound as if they're coming to us straight from a church sanctuary, leading the congregation in a sing-along. West's version evokes the wistful longing of the song—the gently pressing desire to look upward and away from this world of toil and troubles and to fly with all dispatch to a heavenly realm where we'll no longer experience those toils and troubles. The penultimate track on the album, "I'll Fly Away" opens ingeniously into "Spaceship," the album's final track, on which West also gestures toward flight; it's a grittier song—with lyrics delivered in a sing-song fashion—about looking upward to another world to escape the work of this one: "I've been workin' this grave shift and I ain't made shit / I wish I could buy me a spaceship and fly past the sky."

"Spaceship" is a secular hymn that deepens the meaning of "I'll Fly Away," even as it expresses more explicitly the shortcomings, injustices, and inequities of this world. Where "I'll Fly Away" looks beyond this one to a more idealized world, "Spaceship" affirms that no world is ideal, even a heavenly one, so we must accept such flaws and participate in making our own freedom ("buying a spaceship"). Despite its lyrical differences, West's "Spaceship" captures the frustrations that the author of "I'll Fly Away" was feeling when he wrote the song.

Young Albert Brumley loved to sing, and his bass voice boomed loudly when he sang in church. Even though he grew up as a sharecropper's son in rural Oklahoma, picking cotton on his father's farm, he found ways to liven up his life with music. His father played the fiddle, so music always floated through the social gatherings of friends who would make their way to the Brumley farm after a day of work in the fields. As a teenager, he dreamed of one day composing gospel songs. He always carried a pencil and scraps of paper with him so he could write down verses that came to him. When he was sixteen, he wrote his first song, "I Can Hear Them Singing Over There," and a year later, he was attending singing schools and learning more about composing and singing gospel songs.

As a teenager, he spent a few years studying at various singing schools with well-known instructors such as Homer Rodeheaver, Virgil Stamps, and E. M. Bartlett. When Brumley was twenty-one, Bartlett, who wrote the popular gospel song "Victory in Jesus" and who owned the Hartford Music Company, took in Brumley as a student at the Hartford Musical Institute and worked closely with him. Brumley soon started teaching at the Hartford Institute and writing songs prolifically. He likely wrote over six hundred songs, more than one hundred of which were recorded by various artists ranging from Southern gospel quartets such as the Chuck Wagon Gang and the Oak Ridge Boys to Elvis Presley and Ray Charles and the Ray Charles Singers. In addition to "I'll Fly Away," Brumley wrote songs that have become standards of gospel music, such as "Turn Your Radio On," "I'll Meet You in the Morning," "Jesus Hold My Hand," and "If We Never Meet Again." Later, Brumley established his own music company and purchased Hartford Music Company.

Although "I'll Fly Away" became one of the most-recorded gospel songs, Brumley had a far more mundane thought when he came up with his earliest version: to "fly away" from his work. Tired and sweaty and weary from picking cotton on his father's tenant farm day after day in the hot Oklahoma sun, he looked up in the sky and thought about how wonderful it would be if he could fly away from his toils. As he was thinking, the words of a then-popular song, "If I Had the Wings of an Angel (The Prisoner's Song)," came to mind: "Now if I had the wings like an angel / Over these prison walls I would fly / And I'd fly to the arms of my darling / And there I'd be willing to die." At that moment, Brumley thought of his life as a prison from which he wanted to fly like an angel, and this verse gave him the image for his own song in which a bird flies over "these prison walls." Brumley wrote "I'll Fly Away" when he was twenty-four, though he kept revising it before the Hartford Music Company published the song three years later. "I'll Fly Away" is a gospel standard, with thousands of recorded versions, including—in addition to Kanye West's recording—versions by soul singer Aretha Franklin, folk singer Carolyn Hester, country singers Andy Griffith and Crystal Gayle, blues singer Reverend Gary Davis, and the bluegrass group The Dillards, among many others.

"I'LL FLY AWAY"

Like many gospel songs, "I'll Fly Away" depicts a desire to leave the weary struggles of life in this world behind and to move on to a world marked by joy, glorious beauty, and the absence of struggle. Many Christians believe that freedom from such things will come only after death, when the body takes the form of an angel and joins other celestial forms hovering in God's presence in the new city that Revelation 21:1–4 promises:

> Then I saw a new heaven and a new earth; for the first heaven and the first earth had passed away, and the sea was no more. And I saw the holy city, new Jerusalem, coming down out of heaven from God, prepared as a bride adorned for her husband; and I heard a loud voice from the throne saying, "Behold, the dwelling of God is with men. He will dwell with them, and they shall be his people, and God him-self will be with them; he will wipe away every tear from their eyes, and death shall be no more, neither shall there be mourning nor crying nor pain any more, for the former things have passed away."

The expectation of a life free from the shadows of despair, anxiety, suffering, and death fills faithful individuals with hope. They look to the promise of another realm, filled with new possibilities, and sing jubilantly of a day when they'll travel as quickly as they can to leave behind the travails of this world. The song's refrain conveys both the praise and acclamation—"Hallelujah"—that flying away to the "celestial shore" brings, as well as the acceptance that this migration will occur in due time—"by and by." For these reasons, "I'll Fly Away" is one of the gospel songs most often sung at funerals.

The sonic resonance of "I'll Fly Away" derives from its simple lyrical structure. In "I'll Fly Away" the chorus announces the song's theme, circling back on itself over and over to fuel rejoicing in souls and hearts of anyone singing it. As with other gospel songs, repetition is the key to layering a message of hope and beauty and redemption, and the chorus, repeated at least five times, provides the sonic structure for a message of joyous expectation. The chorus itself offers a capsule-like view of the entire song, conveying a sense of flight and the joyousness of this leave-taking: "I'll fly away, oh glory."

The second line in the chorus acknowledges the temporal character of this flight, embracing the light and brightness of the time of day when such flight occurs: "I'll fly away in the morning." A new day dawns with every morning, and so the hope of starting a new life rings loudest in the morning, when the light of new possibility shines brightest. The last two lines of the chorus utter praise for the leave-taking of this life that death brings. This line accepts death as a kind of prerequisite for passing on to a more glorious celestial realm, even celebrating death by acknowledging that there is no pain and suffering in death, but only promise and hope: "When I die, Hallelujah, by and by / I'll fly away."

The song's opening verse plays on the images of brightness, evoking the brilliance of the light that guides us as we fly away from our weary world. The first line conveys a paradox: "Some bright morning when this life is over." Are mornings that bring the darkness of death ever "bright mornings"? How can the light of life shine on a morning when "life is over"? How can one, or does one, celebrate such brightness? From where does such brightness come? In the first, place, "bright morning" simply describes the light spilling out into a new day. Darkness is broken as the sun's rays peek through the veil of night. The light of a new day ushers in hope. In the second place, the brightness of the morning comes not just from the sun's rays; the brightness comes directly from the promise that death brings to carry us to a new world that is filled with light. Here, *bright* can also mean "happy" or "fortunate," for it's on this morning that the singer begins her final journey to the dazzling brilliance of the "home on God's celestial shore." The final image—"God's celestial shore"—outshines all bright lights in this world. The morning is bright because the singer begins her journey to an even more brilliant and brighter morning in an extra-terrestrial realm where the stars and sun outshine any earthly lights. The refrain—"I'll fly away," which floats through each verse two times—urges us to embrace the call to travel from the brightness of this world to the brilliance of the heavenly realm.

The second verse of "I'll Fly Away" also plays on the image of light, but it introduces another image that evokes the limitations and constraints of life in this world. The first line of the verse plays darkness against light—"When the shadows of this life have gone"—unveiling the path to God's celestial shore. As long as we live in the shadows, we are unable to see God clearly, and this life casts many shadows—doubt, fear, anxiety—on our faith in God's sustaining power. When God's light casts out those shadows, when those shadows have gone, we can see our way clearly

to fly to God's celestial shore. Moreover, for many Christian traditions, our bodies are shadows that veil our souls, preventing our
souls from flying to become one with God, the Oversoul, or the
heavenly soul. Thus, when death frees our souls from our bodies,
we can fly toward our homes on "God's celestial shore."

The third line of this verse emphasizes the theme of freedom
that flows through "I'll Fly Away": "Like a bird from these prison
walls I'll fly." Our bodies and our lives imprison us in suffering,
and as long as we trudge through this life, we'll not be able to
free ourselves from the forces—internal or external—that are the
sources of our suffering. This should expand how any Christian
looks on Revelation 21:1–4. Much as Albert Brumley did so may
years ago as he was picking cotton, we look to the only earthly
creatures we know that have wings and that can fly high above
this earth—birds. In our imprisoned states, we marvel at the
freedom of birds, and we declare that we'll be free and fly like
a bird once we escape from these shadows and the prison walls
of our bodies. This freedom also can come when we learn to live
with more joy and gratitude, and less drudgery and focus on the
temporal. When the light dawns on that "bright morning," and
when we fly beyond and high above "these prison walls," we'll fly
away to "God's celestial shore."

The theme of freedom flows into the third verse of "I'll Fly
Away." The persistent images of this famous gospel song are
chains and wings. One cannot fly so long as one is bound and
shackled to this earth. Individuals yearn for freedom and chafe
against the shackles that hold them back, and down, from
achieving it. Various forces chain us to the earth—suffering,

despair, depression, illness, anxiety, social structures—and often, try as we might, we find that it's impossible to break those chains. Individuals are also enslaved by cultural forces beyond their own control; thus, when whites enacted their hatred of blacks by putting the blacks in shackles, lynching them, or controlling their movements—and much of this treatment of blacks by whites continues into the twenty-first century—blacks were physically enslaved and unable to fly away to freedom.

Brumley may not have had such concerns in mind when he wrote "I'll Fly Away," but one of the earliest recordings of the song by the Selah Jubilee Singers allows us to hear these echoes of freedom from physical enslavement, just as other versions allow us to hear echoes of the freedom from spiritual enslavement. Only when individual and social structures are broken, physically and spiritually, can anyone fly freely. The strength to break these shackles arises out of the desire to fly away to another world, a world in which the forces that enslave bodies and souls no longer exist. In this verse when the singer breaks free and has "no more cold iron shackles on my feet," he will be "happy and glad when" he meets God and the other souls who have escaped their shackles and flown to this new world of brilliant light and spiritual freedom.

The song's final verse returns to the anticipation that the weariness and suffering, the enslavement and the persecution, of this world will very soon be over. The happiness that underlies the entire song—words such as *joys, happy, bright,* and *Hallelujah* define the tone of the song—will soon be complete because the days are short until we meet God in that bright and brilliant realm unmarked by sorrow and suffering. The final verse promises that the "home on God's celestial shore" will be "a land where joys will never end." It's a world where we'll be "glad and happy" when "we meet." "I'll Fly Away" counsels us not to be afraid of death, for death transports us to a world in which we are truly free: from the prisons of our bodies and the social structures, sufferings, and sorrows that hold us down. Death is the ultimate act of flying away, so we can look forward to it and embrace it with joy in our hearts and a shout of Hallelujah on our lips.

REFLECTION

There are more than one thousand recordings of "I'll Fly Away." Bluegrass versions of the song tend to be sprightly and jubilantly capture the joy of the song. The Selah Jubilee Singers' version of "I'll Fly Away" is a spirited call-and-response rendition that captures not only the joy of the song but also its insistent, urgent tone. Johnny Cash's almost plain-spoken delivery lends the song a matter-of-factness that is missing in other versions. He delivers a spare rendition that draws attention to the lyrics and draws us into the thematic power of the song. The Dirty Dozen Brass Band delivers a joyous New Orleans marching band–style rendition of the song; their version captures, more than many others, the feeling of a singer running jubilantly to meet his death so that he can fly away to the sweet light of another land. In Aretha Franklin's treatment of "I'll Fly Away" —which she sang at the funeral for Princess Diana—she offers a spaciousness in her phrasing that allows us inside the song as we contemplate its lyrics; her version is marked by celebratory contemplation and acceptance and praise. Southern country gospel artists the Chuck Wagon Gang offer a spacious a cappella version of the song that captures its sonic resonance.

Choose one of these versions of "I'll Fly Away," and listen to Alfred Brumely's gospel song. Reflect for a moment on the lyrics. What does it mean to you to "fly away"? What would that involve for you? Do you believe that you can "fly away"? Do you have hope in a "home on God's celestial shore"? What does such a home look like in your mind? Do you live your life as if death is the "bright morning" on which you will "fly away" to a bright, heavenly realm? Do you believe your body is a prison and that only death will release you from it? What is your view of eternal life? Is there a heavenly realm where "joys will never end"? Where in this world do you see darkness and shadows and imprisonment and enslavement? Can the promise of a "home on God's celestial shore" alleviate those situations of darkness, shadows, imprisonment, and enslavement that plague you? Does the song give you hope? Does it bolster or alter your beliefs about eternal life? In what ways does "I'll Fly Away" resonate with you?

"I'll Fly Away" challenges us to embrace and accept death as a stage along our life's journey that leads us into a brighter and freer place. Whether or not we believe that there is literally a heaven in the sky, the song encourages us to accept death as a liberating event that takes us, literally, out of ourselves. The song challenges us, also, to look beyond ourselves and to see others around us who might be shackled by their sufferings—physical, spiritual, financial, or cultural—and to help them fly away by embracing them with love and giving them hope that there are ways in which they can be free from their shackles. For these reasons, "I'll Fly Away" is a spiritual that will change your life.

THIRTEEN
WHAT A FRIEND WE HAVE IN JESUS

———————

BACKGROUND

WHEN I PLAYED GUITAR, sang, and led music in prisons, one of the favorite and most requested songs was "What a Friend We Have in Jesus." The tune uplifts with its shuffling, ever circling, rhythmic pattern, and the words comfort and assure that, even when the world looks the bleakest, Jesus will always be our best friend to whom we can take our troubles. The congregations in prison sang it the loudest and with more conviction than any other songs we sang. Singing "What a Friend We Have in Jesus" offered those in the group on Sunday mornings a way to assuage the loneliness of prison, the lack of any true or authentic community, and the absence of deep friendships. Along with "Leaning on the Everlasting Arms," whose musical structure also uplifts with its lively rhythms, "What a Friend We Have in Jesus" provided momentary hope to these men that they could find a friend—Jesus—to whom they could confide their troubles and whose friendship would not be fleeting but would endure as they encountered trials and tribulations, even after they were released from prison.

Because "What a Friend We Have in Jesus" provides comfort for those who sing it and hear it, it's perhaps no surprise that the author of the song wrote it as a way of providing comfort to his mother. Joseph Scriven led a life filled with unfortunate circumstances. When he was twenty-four, his fiancé drowned the night before their wedding. Twelve years later, the woman he was supposed to marry fell ill and died before their marriage. When he was twenty-five, Scriven left his native Ireland to move to Canada, in part because of his religious commitment to the Plymouth Brethren community. While he was in Canada, his mother fell gravely ill, so he wrote her a little poem that he titled "Pray without Ceasing" and sent it to her, hoping to comfort her. Scriven wrote the poem with only an audience of one in mind, but it was published later in a newspaper. When Dwight Moody's song leader Ira Sankey discovered it, he asked Charles Crozat Converse, an attorney who also composed songs, to write the music for the song. "What a Friend We Have in Jesus" became a popular gospel song, and it was translated into numerous languages, reaching around the world with its message of comfort and hope. Over the years, "What a Friend We Have in Jesus" has been recorded by musicians as diverse as Bing Crosby and Rosemary Clooney, Glen Campbell and Aretha Franklin, and Ike and Tina Turner and Brad Paisley.

"WHAT A FRIEND WE HAVE IN JESUS"

We don't often associate soul singers Ike and Tina Turner with gospel music. We're more familiar with Tina Turner's growling and soaring vocals in songs such as "Mamma Tell Him," "Don't Play Cheap," or "Proud Mary," and Ike Turner's screaming guitar licks in "Rocket 88," which is often considered the first rock-and-roll song. In 1974, though, the husband-and-wife duo released a gospel album, *The Gospel According to Ike and Tina*. They delivered funky, joyous versions of songs such as "Take My Hand, Precious Lord," "Amazing Grace," and "What a Friend We Have in Jesus." Horns, synthesizers, and swelling background vocals float around and beneath Ike's crunchy guitar as Tina's vocals circle higher and higher and the music ascends to glorious heights. The Turners' version of "What a Friend We Have in Jesus" opens with bass-like synthesizer notes, under which a tambourine shivers. After the opening bars, Tina Turner shouts out the song's opening line—"What a friend we have in Jesus"—as she leads the background singers and the band on a breathless vamp through the rest of the song. The basses punctuate Turner's soul shouts on the verses with their thumping and swooping refrain: "Take it to the Lord in prayer." This version of the song is a soul shaker, and the praise and joy shimmer off the song like heat rising off the asphalt. The Turners deliver a propulsive, stirring, uplifting anthem, urging us to get up and take our woes, our loneliness, and our weariness to Jesus in prayer—and to do it right now!

"What a Friend We Have in Jesus" takes its title from the song's first line, but it lacks the refrain or chorus that provides many gospel songs with their structure. The song has three verses—and sometimes a fourth verse is added—through which the line "Take it to the Lord in prayer" echoes, counseling listeners to action and comforting them in the knowledge that they have a place to which they can carry their troubles. The song builds layer by layer from an initial verse that identifies Jesus as the friend who always listens to our prayers and encourages us not to suffer because we neglect to take our concerns to Jesus, to an enumeration of the kinds of concerns that we can take to Jesus.

The first verse of "What a Friend We Have in Jesus" boldly announces one of the characteristics of Jesus that we often overlook or that we never embrace: his friendship. The song exclaims with wonder and awe "What a friend we have in Jesus," as if to say, "how wonderful, how marvelous" it is that we have a friend in Jesus. Yet Jesus's friendship is hardly a sentimental camaraderie modeled on human friendships, which can be flawed and which can be broken by mistrust or marred by disappointment. Jesus's friendship is marked by his willingness to share our hardships, to bear our sins, our griefs, and our trials with us. Even more, our friend Jesus intercedes with God on our behalf. Through our prayers, we can reveal any pain, any shortcomings, or any trials to Jesus, and he will carry them to God for us. We need not be worried or anxious, for when we turn to our friend Jesus, we can count on him to listen carefully to us, to understand us, and then to transmit our prayers. The second line of the opening verse defines the kind of friend Jesus is: he is the friend who bears all our sins and griefs. In the next two lines, the song emphasizes just how marvelous and astonishing this friendship is—"what a privilege to carry"—and the extent to which Jesus goes for us, carrying everything to God in prayer. The last four lines of the first verse of the song remind us that we often miss out on the blessings of a friendship with Jesus by not sharing our burdens with him so he can intercede on our behalf: "Oh, what peace we often forfeit / Oh, what needless pain we bear" because we do not carry everything to God in prayer.

The second verse of "What a Friend We Have in Jesus" counsels us never to be discouraged when we have Jesus as our friend. As long as we "take it to the Lord in prayer," we can find peace and comfort no matter how challenging our trials might be. The verse opens with two straightforward questions that involve individuals and communities: "Have we trials and temptations? / Is there trouble anywhere?" Even in the most trying times—whether we are reeling from the death of a loved one or we are tempted to shatter relationships through broken trust or to follow our temptations to question our faith—we can find a faithful friend in Jesus with whom we can honestly share the challenges we are facing. The second part of the verse reiterates Jesus's faithfulness, providing insight into the way that Jesus can be such a good friend. Jesus is a "friend so faithful" who will "all our sorrows share" because Jesus, having lived a life like ours, knows the temptations we confront as human beings, and he "knows our every weakness." Because we have such an intimate friendship with Jesus, we should never be reluctant—no matter how discouraged or sad or anxious we are—to share our sorrows, our trials, our shortcomings, our temptations, or our doubts with our friend Jesus.

The third verse of "What a Friend We Have in Jesus" intensifies the theme and message of the first two verses, and it adds a beautiful affirmation of the intimacy of our friendship with Jesus. The first lines sound the familiar note: "Are we weak and heavy-laden, / Cumbered with a load of care?" Heavy burdens— the times we feel as if we have failed, the losses we carry with us—weigh us down in our lives and weaken us so that we're often unable to face the challenges of daily life. In our weakness, we also might make decisions about our relationships, our jobs, or our faith that have disastrous consequences, thus leaving us with a burden of brokenness or guilt or doubt. We might also be weak from illness or desperate hunger and thirst, and our bodies carry the weight of these sufferings. We often look for a place where we can find comfort and strength; we can find them in our friendship with Jesus, which this verse describes as a refuge: "Precious Savior, still our refuge." The beauty of this single line lies in its promise of a safe place, a refuge, and its promise that this safe place is everlasting ("still"). We can always rest in the arms of Jesus, for Jesus is always with us. No matter what happens in our lives, his arms encircle and enfold us in love: "In His arms He'll take and shield thee."

This verse describes one more situation in which Jesus offers comfort: the loss of friendship—"Do thy friends despise, forsake thee?" This line can refer either to broken friendships that we have caused through our own actions or to those friendships that fall apart because of our strong Christian faith. Our friends might forsake us when they learn how deeply we embrace Christianity and try to live by its principles as we understand them. Yet Jesus never forsakes us nor despises us; like a true friend, he takes us in his arms and shields us so that we will "find a solace there." We need simply to remember that Jesus is our everlasting friend who shelters us from all trials and sorrows, as well as the one who intercedes for us. We need simply, according to the song, to carry all our burdens to our friend, who will then carry them to God.

Some more recent versions of "What a Friend We Have in Jesus" add a fourth verse, which is not found in Scriven's original poem and which is left out of most hymnals. This verse sings of a time when we'll no longer need to pray. The verse reiterates the themes of the other three verses—bringing all our burdens to God in prayer—but then looks to a time when we'll see God face-to-face, so there will no longer be a "need for prayer"; for "soon in glory bright, unclouded" we'll participate in "rapture, praise, and endless worship," and that "will be our sweet portion there."

"What a Friend We Have in Jesus" is a comforting and reassuring song, encouraging us to embrace the refuge of a friend who is willing to listen as we share our troubles and who understands our weaknesses. This friend never condemns us, forsakes us, or despises us; our friend Jesus welcomes us with open arms, consoles and comforts us, and intercedes for us.

REFLECTION

We don't often think of Jesus as a friend, probably because when we think of him this way, it makes him less divine and more human. It makes him more like us, and we often reject the idea that Jesus could have had trials and temptations and cares or that he was ever weighed down by heavy burdens. Our human definition of friendship, we feel, could never describe adequately the relationship we have with Jesus, who bore our sins and died for us, and so we could never feel for Jesus what we might feel for a friend. Thinking of Jesus as a friend pulls him down to our level, so we often have difficulty calling Jesus our friend or treating Jesus as our friend.

Yet "What a Friend We Have in Jesus" boldly encourages us to embrace Jesus as our friend, for unlike our other friends, Jesus never forsakes us and always welcomes us with open arms, even when we make mistakes or when we fail. Jesus can comfort us when we're lonely, heal us when we're sick, encourage us when we're feeling weak, bolster us when we're doubting, and intercede always for us with God, as long as we share our prayers with him.

Listen to several different versions of "What a Friend We Have in Jesus." What are some of the differences you hear in these versions? Which of these versions speaks most to you and encourages you? Which of these versions best underscores the central themes of the song? Does an upbeat and funky version such as Ike and Tina Turner's rendition capture the joyous character of the song? Or does a slower, more measured rendition, such as country singer Alan Jackson's version, come closer to capturing the song's focus on the intimacy of friendship? Select one version of the song that speaks most to you, and listen to it in a meditative fashion. What themes emerge from the song for you? Do you feel the intimacy of Jesus's friendship? Can you imagine Jesus taking you in his arms and holding you close to comfort you? Can you be comfortable enough to share all your troubles in your prayer and with Jesus, your friend? In what ways does "What a Friend We Have in Jesus" inspire you? Do you find comfort and solace in this song?

"What a Friend We Have in Jesus" moves us to think anew about our relationship with Jesus; the music itself is bright and uplifting and carries us out of ourselves as we think about our relationship with Jesus. The lyrics spiral upward, reminding us of Jesus's love and care for us and of his being with us always. Whether we accept his friendship or not, Jesus remains loyal and loving to us, and when we remember this, we will find comfort. For these reasons, "What a Friend We Have in Jesus" is a gospel song that will change your life.

Fourteen

BRETHREN, WE HAVE MET TO WORSHIP

BACKGROUND

M ANY CHRISTIANS first heard the song "Brethren, We Have Met to Worship" at a camp meeting or a tent revival. In the 1960s and 1970s, many Christian artists, including contemporary stars Cynthia Clawson and Sandi Patty, recorded versions of the song, and the song is often used by contemporary praise bands to call congregations to worship. Hundreds of versions of the song are available—from instrumentals to bluegrass versions to Southern gospel quartet versions to choruses or groups singing the song in its shape-note setting. But its first publication was likely in 1829; and since that time, "Brethren, We Have Met to Worship" has always been a staple of Southern gospel music.

As with many gospel songs, once again, we know very little about the details of this one's composition. It first appeared in a collection of hymns published in 1819, where the lyrics were attributed to George T. Atkins. Atkins was born in England, but migrated to America, where he settled first in Ohio. He served there as a Methodist minister, before moving to east Tennessee, which is where he seems to have written the lyrics for "Brethren, We Have Met to Worship." The folk lyrics did not have a musical setting until ten years later in 1829 when William Moore, about whom we have no information, published the melody "Holy Manna" in a shape-note tunebook, *Columbian Harmony*. Six years later, in 1835, the song was included in a shape-note songbook, *Southern Harmony*, which became a very popular collection that introduced songs to choruses in churches and singing schools, especially in the South. The shape-note method of learning music focused on harmony singing and provided various shapes—a triangle, a circle, a square, for example—that represented notes on the musical scale—fa, mi, sol, la. The version of "Brethren, We Have Met for Worship" found in *Southern Harmony* continues to be popular among many rural congregations in the South that still practice shape-note singing.

Moore's tune of "Holy Manna" transcended the lyrics for "Brethren, We Have Met to Worship," however. His tune has provided the musical settings for numerous hymns, including "God, Who Stretched the Spangled Heavens," "All Who Hunger," "Christians, Let Us Go and Serve Him," and "Gracious God, You Send Great Blessings." In addition to these songs having Moore's "Holy Manna" tune in common with "Brethren, We Have Met to Worship," the lyrics of each take up many of the same themes of "Brethren, We Have Met to Worship": adoration, praise, worship, justice, service, blessings, and communion.

"BRETHREN, WE HAVE MET TO WORSHIP"

Many gospel songs act as calls to worship, as calls to gather congregations together to bring joys, worries, or concerns before the community, as calls for individuals in the community to share their burdens with others and with God. Sometimes congregations sing these songs as they are gathering into the worship space, greeting others as they sing and joining their voices in swelling choruses that shout, "Welcome! We are glad you are here in this place with us to worship God." Many times, these songs evoke communities of ancient worshipers who might have gathered together on the banks of a river, or on a desolate plain, to praise God and give thanks to God for bringing them through trials and tribulations. Songs such as "Brethren, We Have Met to Worship" connect worshiping communities through time and space, recalling earlier times when congregations faced the troubles of their world together and gathered to worship, to pray, to love, and to act, and thus to receive God's blessings. Such songs can create a holy atmosphere, or they can foster a spirit of revival, and "Brethren, We Have Met for Worship" was often sung at camp meetings and tent revivals in the nineteenth and twentieth centuries.

Several lyrics in "Brethren, We Have Met to Worship" connect contemporary congregations to ancient worshiping communities. The clearest connection to ancient communities comes in the refrain, repeated in the last two lines of each verse, in which "holy manna" or "sweet manna" is showered all around. The bread of life that sustained the Israelites in the desert following their escape from Egypt also sustains us and is the gift that God provides every congregation that takes care of the sad, lonely, and anxious among them. Some hymnals even list the song as "Holy Manna," which is the tune for the song. In the third verse, the song invokes "Moses' sisters" as women who came to his need when he was in trouble;

and in the fourth verse, we hear about the "trembling jailer"—a reference to the story of Paul and Silas in Acts 16:24–29—and "weeping Mary"—a reference to Mary weeping at Jesus's Cross— including their troubles and sorrows and their redemption. The song asks some simple questions when it calls up these models: Who among us is like these people? Who among is fearful about the physical and spiritual challenges that every day brings? Who among us is weeping, trembling, struggling, crying? How can we, as the gathered community, help them?

Unlike many gospel songs, "Brethren, We Have Met to Worship" does not proceed in a call-and-response fashion. With such songs, such as "Keep Your Lamps Trimmed and Burning," the song leader or lead singer calls out the main line, or lines, of the song, and the chorus, or the congregation, responds by repeating the line, or by responding to the leader's words with several lines of response. Call-and-response songs spiral upward until they achieve a climax before spiraling back toward a conclusion. "Brethren, We Have Met to Worship" features a refrain—"Brethren, pray, and holy manna will be showered all around" (and the lyrics change slightly in the final verse)— repeated as the last two lines of each verse. While each verse of the song adds layer by layer to the overall theme of the song, each verse focuses on a different theme, adding to the luster and complexity of the song.

One of the liveliest versions of "Brethren, We Have Met to Worship" is by a little-known bluegrass gospel band called the Seminole String Band. Their version opens with a downstroke of the bow on the fiddles before the fiddles scamper off in a sprightly romp through the verses. The guitar and fiddles play call and response underneath the gorgeously lilting harmony vocals; in the first verse the lead singer's voice mimics the fiddles' notes, doubling the vocals with instrument. The Seminole String Band version draws us happily into worship and praise, encouraging us to sing along with them as we joyfully make our way to praise God.

Ken Medema, a Christian artist best known for the prayer chorus "Lord, Listen to Your Children Praying," delivers a fiery, rollicking version of "Brethren, We Have Met to Worship." His take on the song opens with his characteristically rousing piano chords. He rumbles and rolls the bass chords in the song's introduction before he joins in with his vocals. Medema emphasizes the exalted nature of the lyrics by modulating into a new key after every other verse over his blossoming barrelhouse piano. Medema's version takes us to church, even if we never enter a church's doors, for with just his vocals and his piano—the only two instruments in the song, with the possible exception of a xylophone—he creates a sacred space, inviting us into it to dance and celebrate God's goodness and mercy and love.

The first verse very simply calls the community to worship and to enter the place where the community finds God: we have "met to worship and adore the Lord our God." Adoration is a key part of worship—not adoration in the sense of adoring a puppy or a lover, but adoration in the sense of standing in the face of mystery with awe and wonder—namely, contemplating the depth of the mystery of God's presence. To adore God, we must be in a certain state of mind, and so worshiping God requires that we pray for the Spirit of God to move us and to open our minds to listen for God's words as we listen to the preacher "preach the word." The first verse emphasizes that "all is vain, unless the Spirit of the Holy One comes down," so the verse implores members of the community to pray—another essential act of worship—so that the Holy Spirit will enliven every element of worship. The result of praying, preaching, and the movement of the Spirit—but especially praying—is that every member of the community will be nourished and sustained: "holy manna will be showered all around."

Even in the midst of worship, though, individuals become aware of their shortcomings, their failings, their sins—or individuals enter worship deeply aware of such shortcomings. In the same way, the three center verses of the song focus on several such themes. First, "Brethren, We Have Met for Worship" recognizes that "poor sinners" are all around, and that they are "trembling on the brink of woe." The contrast between the rewards of salvation and the punishments of sin flows through the entire song, and the second verse illustrates this contrast dramatically. Sinners are "trembling," "sinking down," and "death is coming, hell is moving" for these individuals. Even more dramatically, the song asks the gathered worshipers to look around at their family members—fathers, mothers, children—and asks if we can bear to see them sink down into hell for their sinfulness. When congregations sing this song today, the often-somber tone of the piano or organ and the often-solemn singing of the choir enable us to focus on the moving beauty of the music so that we very seldom consider the lyrics. Even in bluegrass versions of the song, the sprightly music skitters along so that we get caught up in the pace of the tune and don't hear the verses about sin, hell, and salvation; instead, we think the song is mainly about the beauties of worship.

Second, in the middle verses the members of the congregation—and in the third verse the "sisters," rather than the "brethren"—are implored to "help" those struggling with sin, who are called "trembling mourners" in this verse, and to witness to them, testifying to them about the power of God to save their souls: "Tell them all about the Savior." The theme of witnessing, or testifying, to the power of God in one's life—to proclaim, "See what the Lord has done for me!"—emerges here as a characteristic part of worship. In this view of worship, if we adore God because of God's presence in our lives and the world, and our worship is an aesthetic form of that adoration, then we feel so showered by the beauty of God that we want to share it with others and to persuade them to see and feel what we see and feel. When we witness to others as a part of worship, we can feed others the holy manna that sustains us, and we can be nourished by this same manna that is "showered all around" us. In fact, one way of interpreting these lines is to view the sinners, who have been saved and now been washed white as snow, as the manna—which is symbolically white—that falls around us. In the penultimate verse, the brothers are urged to raise their "cries to help" the "trembling" and "tearful" sinners, and the sisters are urged to let their "prayers abound" for these same sinners.

Finally, the last verse of "Brethren, We Have Met to Worship" shifts the terrain from the earthly community to the heavenly community. To enter the heavenly community, we must "love our

God supremely," "love each other, too," and "love and pray for sinners." We must be active in our earthly communities in these ways until "God makes all things new." When that happens, God will call us to our heavenly home, where Christ will serve us at a banquet table, offering us "sweet manna." Our worship, then, involves more than simply praying and listening to preaching; it involves active and loving service to others, even those we meet inside our worshiping community who might be hurting and trembling with woe, not because they are afraid of hell, but because they have experienced despair or loss.

"Brethren, We Have Met to Worship" might best be described as a hymn rather than a gospel song, even though its themes rise directly from gospel music. When the song is sung by congregations, it is often sung in a stately, slow register to encourage adoration and praise of God, and it thus sounds more like a hymn. Hymns are often described as songs that focus on the adoration and praise of God, while gospel songs focus on human experience. So, when a bluegrass group sings "Brethren, We Have Met to Worship," it often sounds more like a gospel song, not only because of the fast pace of the music, but also because of the focus on the human experiences that serve as the centerpiece of the song.

REFLECTION

When we sing "Brethren, We Have Met to Worship" and listen closely to the words, we might feel as if this song doesn't speak to our experience or to the ways we think experience God and church in the early part of the twenty-first century. The verses about sin and fear of hell, and looking into hell and seeing our closest family members, may not resonate with many contemporary Christians. Preaching about personal sin and salvation, and the punishments and rewards of each, is largely absent from today's Christian worship. Churches often focus on corporate sin—the sins of societies as they oppress and marginalize others, often in the name of God—and corporate salvation instead. Have we lost something important in this? Churches have difficulty articulating a vision of corporate salvation, but it does involve and require loving others as God loves us. If many of the images in "Brethren, We Have Met to Worship" are foreign to contemporary Christians, can the song still reach us emotionally and spiritually?

The sheer beauty of the music of "Brethren, We Have Met to Worship" can transport us whenever we hear it, and the music evokes in us a spirit of worship. Many versions of the song open with spare and stately piano chords that mimic the majesty of God, the Lord God whom the community has met to adore. If we believe that a key element of worship is adoring God, then singing "Brethren, We Have Met to Worship" as an opening song or as an invocation prepares us to worship and opens our hearts to God's majesty. The song asks us to look outside of ourselves and to worship the God who creates, nourishes, and sustains us. The tune for the song, "Holy Manna," also provides the musical setting for "God, Who Stretched the Spangled Heavens," a 1967 hymn of adoration and creation that praises God's creative activity, which illustrates that the tune itself transcends time and place with its beauty.

"Brethren, We Have Met to Worship" also encourages us to look outside ourselves and to love others as God loves us. Even if we're not looking around us for the "trembling sinner," as the song urges, we can look around us to see who is crying, who is hurting, who is mourning, who is angry, who is despondent, who is anxious, or who is fearful. We can pray with all our power for those individuals; we can share with them the times we have experienced God's power in our lives; we can show them the beauty of God by being the face of God to them. Most importantly, we can introduce them to a community of individuals who, like them, continue to deal every day with fear, loss, distress, and disappointment.

"Brethren, We Have Met to Worship" encourages us to embrace community, to adore the majesty of the God who has created the beautiful community in which we uphold each other, and to share with each other the nourishing and sustaining rewards of living life together—"sweet manna"—as we worship God together. "Brethren, We Have Met to Worship" redeems us, evoking the beauty and the spirit of love in our worship of God and service to others. For these reasons, "Brethren, We Have Met to Worship" is a gospel song that can change our lives.

FIFTEEN
STEAL AWAY TO JESUS

BACKGROUND

MANY SPIRITUALS AND GOSPEL SONGS arise out of a longing for a life free from oppression and suffering. Some songs focus on individual bondage to sin and suffering—"Amazing Grace," for example, deals, at least on one level, with a person's wretched feelings about himself and the deliverance he receives through God's grace. Other songs, meanwhile, deal with excruciating loss—"Precious Lord, Take My Hand," for example—and the enduring search for God's comforting touch. Still others focus on God's greatness—"How Great Thou Art"—or the exalted character of worship—"Brethren, We Have Met to Worship."

The predominate theme in many spirituals and gospel songs is the longing for an otherworldly existence, one that is marked by enduring love, joy, peace, and hope that is absent in this world. Sometimes these songs depict an apocalyptic scene in which an otherworldly kingdom—the kingdom of heaven—awaits those who are prepared to enter it, as does "Keep Your Lamps Trimmed and Burning." There is an entire group of spirituals, though, that deal with the theme of escape to a better world than this one and often double as messages to groups of slaves about a literal escape to another world. We've already looked at a few of these (which are often attributed to Harriet Tubman), such as "Swing Low,

Sweet Chariot," "Wade in the Water," and "Many Thousand Gone"; now we will explore "Steal Away to Jesus."

Just as with "Swing Low, Sweet Chariot," the origins of "Steal Away to Jesus" are uncertain. Unlike "Swing Low, Sweet Chariot," though, "Steal Away to Jesus" does not feature a call-and-response structure outside of the refrain, at least in its earliest versions. Shirley Caesar and Michelle Williams's version, however, adds extra lyrics to the original and features a lively sing-song call-and-response second and final refrain that shouts, "Steal away!" and "Steal away home!" repeatedly.

"Steal Away to Jesus" is very likely another of those spirituals that was passed down among slaves who first sang it to one another to advise others on how to steal away, possibly run away, and escape to their true home—whether their heavenly home or simply a new home across the river—where they will be free from slavery. The final line of the refrain—"I ain't got long to stay here"—signals the expectation that this journey to a another and better world will happen soon. Like "Swing Low, Sweet Chariot," "Steal Away to Jesus" has occasionally been attributed to the previously mentioned Wallace Willis, born in Mississippi, the slave of an owner who was at least half-Choctaw. Also like "Swing Low, Sweet Chariot," "Steal Away to Jesus" became a popular song during the Civil Rights Movement in the American 1950s and '60s.

The Fisk Jubilee Singers made perhaps the earliest recording of the spiritual in 1915, and since then artists from Mahalia Jackson and Nat King Cole to Paul Robeson and Elijah Caldwell, the Soul Stirrers, and Caesar and Williams, among others, have recorded it.

"STEAL AWAY TO JESUS"

What does it mean to "steal away to Jesus"? On one level, stealing away involves running away stealthily, but on another level to steal away to Jesus is to die and to go to heaven to live a life at Jesus's side. "Steal Away to Jesus" operates on both levels, exhorting its listeners to slip away stealthily from their owners and escape, while also counseling them to look beyond this world to heaven and the new life with Jesus. The song opens with the refrain whose final line floats through the song's verses to remind listeners and singers that their lives in this world won't last long. Most versions of the song open slowly and sparely, and this stately, almost somber tone continues through the rest of the song. The refrain simply repeats the exhortation: "Steal away, steal away, steal away to Jesus! / Steal away, steal away home / I ain't got long to stay here."

The first verse of "Steal Away to Jesus" opens with the line: "My Lord, He calls me," conveying a surrender to the call of Jesus to steal away to the home—in this case, the eternal or heavenly home—mentioned in the refrain. Jesus's call to the singers is accompanied both by a theophany—God's revelation in a natural event, such as a thunderstorm—and by a trumpet sound in the second and third lines in the first verse: "He calls me by the thunder / The trumpet sounds within my soul." The song draws its biblical imagery of the thunder from the storms in which God reveals God's self to God's community. In Exodus 20:18 God's delivery of the Ten Commandments is accompanied by thunder and lightning: "When all the people perceived the thunderings and the lightnings and the sound of the trumpet and the mountain smoking, the people were afraid and trembled." Similarly, in the New Testament, 1 Corinthians 15:51–52 witnesses to the change from the material to the spiritual, which is accompanied by the sound of a trumpet: "We shall all be changed, in a moment, in the twinkling of an eye, at the last trumpet. For the trumpet will sound, and the dead will be raised imperishable, and we shall be changed." These two lines in the song depict the singers stealing away to an eternal world beyond this material world, and the last line of the verse conveys that this journey will happen soon.

If "Steal Away to Jesus" contains coded messages to slaves about escaping to free lands, then the first verse may depict a slave owner calling to a slave in anger ("by the thunder"). The slave, however, hears the signals from those working in the Underground Railroad ("the trumpet sounds") and prepares to follow that signal. The slave yearns to follow that sound as soon as he can so that he can steal away to this new home, for he doesn't want to remain in the same land as an angry and vindictive owner.

The second verse of "Steal Away to Jesus" continues the nature imagery of the first verse: "Green trees are bending / Poor sinners are trembling." From a spiritual perspective, the trees are the individuals in the community who are bending to God's will; these individuals admit their shortcomings—"poor sinners"— and they shake and tremble with delight and awe as they prepare themselves to steal away to their heavenly home. Their trembling comes not from fear but from the anxious expectation that they will soon be able to leave this world and join other Christians in their heavenly home. These two lines acknowledge that the singers and listeners hope that they'll be united with their families and friends with Jesus in this other world.

The last two lines of the second verse repeat the refrain of the sounding trumpet—the resonance of the individual's soul with the souls of others—and the loud call that the singers don't have long to be in this world. On another level, the green trees bending and poor sinners trembling could be references to slaves who are being whipped for their shortcomings; or it is possible that they are being whipped by their owner because the owner has discovered their plans to escape. The sound of the trumpet—the call of the workers on the Underground Railroad to freedom—gives them hope that they can still steal away soon to a home where they will not face this punishment. The green trees could also be images of the woods separating the slaves' present home from the home where they will be free; the trembling could be the fear and excitement of moving through these woods to their new home.

Another theophany occurs in the song's third verse: "My Lord, He calls me / He calls me by the lightning." Once again God calls the singers home in dramatic fashion, revealing God's self in a dazzling and brilliant light that shows the slaves the path to their heavenly home. The lightning is once again accompanied by the sound of the trumpet in the souls of the singers and listeners. The trumpet of the Lord resonates within the one waiting for the call to follow its sound. On another level, the lightning could be the wrath of the owner flashing out at the slave, who hears instead the sound of an eternal world calling to him. Or the lightning may also be the torches held by workers in the Underground Railroad, lighting the path through the darkness of the woods for those escaping the harsh and degrading conditions of their slavery.

Shirley Caesar and Michelle Williams add lyrics to their version of "Steal Away to Jesus" that convey the urgency of the song. They turn the song into a call-and-response gospel song in which one singer will call out the phrase, "Steal away," while the other responds with the times when and the reasons why one needs to steal away to Jesus: "(Steal away) In the midnight hour / (Steal away) When you need some power / (Steal away) When you heart is heavy / (Steal away to Jesus) Steal away to Jesus / (Steal away) Steal away, steal away / Steal away home (Steal away home) / Haven't got long / (I haven't got long) / To stay here (To stay here)." In their version, "Steal Away to Jesus" takes on an immediacy with our desire to run away to world where we'll no longer be heavy-hearted and where we'll no longer face the darkness of the "midnight hour," when the blackness of our suffering is the most insufferable. According to this verse, we also steal away when we "need some power" of God to guide and direct and strengthen us. This version of the spiritual movingly reveals to us the reasons we should steal away to Jesus, and soon.

REFLECTION

How do our lives change if we take the words and themes of "Steal Away to Jesus" to heart? What happens when we "run to Jesus," escaping the harshness and suffering of this world, in search of a new world where we'll no longer face such suffering? How do the worlds in which we live throw up obstacles to stealing away to Jesus? How many times do we express the hope that we could steal away to Jesus, escaping this world through death and living by the side of Jesus in a heavenly realm? When is the last time you wanted to "steal away to Jesus"? What made you want to do so?

Listen to two versions of "Steal Away to Jesus": the Mahalia Jackson and Nat King Cole version and the Shirley Caesar and Michelle Williams version. Other than the lyrical differences, what are the differences you find in each? What about the versions moves you? Think deeply about the musical structure of the song. How does the music itself move you? How does the music invite you into the song, and does the music keep you engaged in the song? What about the lyrics? Which version conveys the themes of the song the most effectively? How relevant is "Steal Away to Jesus" to you today?

"Steal Away to Jesus" inspires us to look beyond our world to the promises of a world in which we can be free of our troubles, trials, and tribulations. While we can't allow ourselves to gaze longingly at an eternal world and neglect the world in which we live, we can embrace the hope, beauty, joy, and love promised by the existence of that other world and live out those qualities in our own world. Stealing away to Jesus doesn't mean losing ourselves in the search for some ethereal world, but it means bringing the qualities of the kingdom of God into this world. The eternal impinges on the ordinary, and the idea of stealing away to Jesus reminds us that by following the example of Jesus, we can change our world into the world of hope, love, and peace that Jesus calls us to make it. "Steal Away to Jesus" is, therefore, a spiritual that can change our lives.

O N HIS 2016 ALBUM *Delilah*, Anderson East delivers a soulful tale of temptation and salvation. In the song, he alludes to the stereotypical Saturday night or Sunday morning theme of gospel music. In "Devil in Me," the singer describes a "girl from Shelbyville / [who] gave her life to Jesus / First Antioch Baptist Church / Where her daddy preaches," who's "pretty as her mama." This angelic creature ("she could be an angel") "brings out the devil in me," according to the singer. He calls her his "Delilah"—a reference to the biblical story of Samson and Delilah in the Old Testament book of Judges, chapter 16—for she's his weakness and she brings him to his knees. The singer pleads for God to forgive him for what he's thinking—"it's Saturday night and I'm high and I've been drinking"—about the preacher's daughter, for on Sunday morning he'll "look over and see her smile" and bow his head when the choir is singing. The song opens with rolling piano chords that underlie many gospel songs, and the chorus features a swelling of voices on which the pleas for forgiveness float; the background singers ascend the higher registers as the singer maintains his lower tones. East's song illustrates the pervasiveness and power of gospel music. While "Devil in Me" showcases the swaying rhythms of Southern soul music—with its punchy horns and soaring vocals—it also offers an example of the far-reaching force of the themes, melodic structures, and sonic harmonies of gospel music.

Of course, you won't find Anderson East on *Billboard*'s gospel or contemporary Christian music charts. (For some inexplicable reason, the magazine established two charts a few years ago: one to track gospel music, which they seem to define as black gospel music; and the second to track contemporary Christian music, which is mostly music by white artists and consists mainly of praise-and-worship music.) Neither will you find Van Morrison, Christine Ohlman, Amy Helm, Mike Farris, Eli "Paperboy" Reed, Ike and Tina Turner (if they were still recording), Rebecca Lynn Howard (listen to her version of Larry Cordle's "Jesus and Bartenders"), Zeshan B, or any number of artists whose music builds on the foundations of gospel music. Yet, once you listen to much of these artists' music, or once you listen to any early rock and roll, you'll hear the mighty strains of gospel music—the swelling B3 organ, the crunchy guitars, the soaring voices of a background chorus lifting the song higher and higher. If you listen closely enough to a song such as the Rolling Stones' "Shine a Light," for example, or The Band's version of Bob Dylan's "I Shall Be Released," or even Dylan's "All Along the Watchtower" (which alludes to Isaiah 21:5–9), you can't help but be moved by the propulsive strains of gospel-inflected music. (I have purposely selected songs that are far outside the musical universe we call "gospel.")

When publisher Jon Sweeney proposed that I write this book, I sent him a list of songs I hoped to cover in these pages. This book could have easily been titled "One Thousand Spirituals That Will Change Your Life." I selected those fifteen songs with which I thought readers would be familiar and have some experience singing. I also chose songs that I have some personal experience with as a musician, playing them in either churches or bars or prisons. Most of these songs are older, but the most contemporary song here—"If Heaven Never Was Promised to Me"—may have had the greatest impact on me, as you know from reading that chapter. When I started playing guitar and singing, I stayed as far away from church music as I could. Over the years that changed, and now when I play at a club, I include at least one song whose sonic structure is shaped by gospel music, recently leading a sing-along of "Will the Circle Be Unbroken?" Gospel music moves and stirs me, and writing this book has given me an opportunity to meditate on some of the reasons that it continues to inspire me. I hope you'll also find inspiration in these songs and start to listen closely to all music to hear the ways in which it can change you.

ACKNOWLEDGMENTS

Whether they know it or not, many people have inspired me to write this book, and to stay with it once I started it.

I want to thank Jon Sweeney, publisher at Paraclete Press, for saying to me, "I have a book you can write." His suggestion came at a difficult time in my life, so I am grateful for his suggestion and for his having faith, and patience, that this is a subject about which I could write.

Numerous musicians have inspired me, whether through conversations or through their music, and this list, I am afraid, will never be complete: Larry Campbell and Teresa Williams, Christine Ohlman, Emily Duff, Wendy Lorraine Colonna, Amy Ray, Beth Nielsen Chapman, Rosanne Cash, Mary Chapin Carpenter, Mary Gauthier, Eliza Gilkyson, Emmylou Harris, Rodney Crowell, Mandy Barnett, Brooke Aldridge, John Oates, Kathy Mattea, Bonnie Bramlett, Candi Staton, and so many others.

I thank my colleagues and friends at *No Depression* who've encouraged me and given me the opportunity to write about some of this music over the years: Stacy Schorr Chandler, Maureen Cross, Kyla Fairchild, Adam Kirr, Sonja Nelson, Kim Ruehl, Hilary Saunders, and Chris Wadsworth.

I thank Brian Schoettler, music director of First United Methodist Church, Evanston, Illinois—and before Brian, Ace Gongoso and David Castillo Gocher—for the opportunity to play this music. Thanks also to my fellow guitarists Jim Niemira and Phil Perry for strumming along.

My gratitude as well to the late Jess Moody, for showing me that being more like Christ means being fully human, and to my mates in the Teens Alive for God Band: George Baldwin—who asked me to join—Lamar Christie, and Lewis Spencer.

I thank Susan Sparks, Larry Russell, Brian Smith, David Cantwell, Barry Mazor, Aaron Cohen, Maria Ivey, Greg Carey, Jewly Hight, Cary Baker, Jim McHolland, and so many other friends for sharing conversations and modeling excellent writing.

I thank copyeditor Shannon Lee for saving me from many infelicities in her close reading of the manuscript.

Thanks to my loving family, who have been patient with me as I worked to complete this book: Sookhee, Joshua, Lianna, and Haley. I couldn't have completed it without their love and support.

I have dedicated this book to my mother, Suetta Tisdale Carrigan, and to the memory of my father, Henry Lowell Carrigan, and my grandparents.

SELECTED READINGS ON GOSPEL MUSIC

Abbington, James. *Let the Church Sing On! Reflections on Black Sacred Music*. Chicago: GIA, 2009.

Boyer, Horace Clarence. *How Sweet the Sound: The Golden Age of Gospel*. Washington, DC: Elliott and Clark, 1995.

Brooks, Tim. *Lost Sounds: Blacks and the Birth of the Recording Industry, 1890–1919*. Urbana: University of Illinois Press, 2004.

Burnim, Mellonee V., and Portia K. Maultsby, eds. *African American Music: An Introduction*. New York: Routledge, 2006.

Butler, Jerry, with Earl Smith. *Only the Strong Survive: Memoirs of a Soul Survivor*. Bloomington: University of Indiana Press, 2000.

Carpenter, Bil. *Uncloudy Days: The Gospel Music Encyclopedia*. San Francisco: Backbeat Books, 2005.

Codohas, Nadine. *Queen: The Life and Music of Dinah Washington*. New York: Pantheon, 2004.

Cohen, Aaron. *Amazing Grace*. New York: Continuum, 2011.

Cone, James. *The Spirituals and the Blues: An Interpretation*. New York: Seabury Press, 1972.

Cusic, Don. *Saved by Song: A History of Gospel and Christian Music*. Jackson: University of Mississippi Press, 2012.

Darden, Robert. *Nothing but Love in God's Water: Black Sacred Music from the Civil War to the Civil Rights Movement*, vol. 1. University Park: Pennsylvania State University Press, 2014.

———. *People Get Ready! A New History of Gospel Music*. New York: Continuum, 2004.

Goff, James R. *Close Harmony: A History of Southern Gospel*. Chapel Hill: University of North Carolina Press, 2002.

Harris, Michael. *The Rise of Gospel Blues: The Music of Thomas Andrew Dorsey in the Urban Church*. Oxford: Oxford University Press, 1992.

Harrison, Douglas. *Then Sings My Soul: The Culture of Southern Gospel Music*. Champaign–Urbana: University of Illinois Press, 2012.

Heilbut, Anthony. *The Fan Who Knew Too Much*. New York: Knopf, 2012.

———. *The Gospel Sound*, 4th ed. New York: Limelight Editions, 1992.

Jackson, Jerma A. *Singing in My Soul: Black Gospel Music in a Secular Age*. Chapel Hill: University of North Carolina Press, 2004.

Jackson, Mahalia, with Evan McLeod Whyte. *Movin' On Up*. New York: Villard, 1966.

Lornell, Kip. *Happy in the Service of the Lord: African-American Sacred Vocal Harmony Quartets in Memphis*, 2nd ed. Knoxville: University of Tennessee Press, 1995.

Marovich, Robert M. *A City Called Heaven: Chicago and the Birth of Gospel Music*. Champaign–Urbana: University of Illinois Press, 2015.

McNeil, W. K., ed. *Encyclopedia of American Music*. New York: Routledge, 2005.

Oliver, Paul, Max Harrison, and William Bolcom. *The New Grove Gospel, Blues, and Jazz.* New York: Norton, 1986.

Pruter, Robert. *Chicago Soul.* Urbana: University of Illinois Press, 1992.

Reagon, Bernice Johnson. *If You Don't Go, Don't Hinder Me: The African American Sacred Song Tradition.* Lincoln: University of Nebraska Press, 2001.

Smith, Ruth A. *The Life and Works of Thomas Andrew Dorsey.* Chicago: Prairie State Press, 1935.

Wald, Gayle F. *Shout, Sister, Shout! The Untold Story of Rock-and-Roll Trailblazer Sister Rosetta Tharpe.* Boston: Beacon Press, 2007.

Wolff, Daniel, with S. R. Crain, Clifton White, and G. David Tennenbaum. *You Send Me: The Life and Times of Sam Cooke.* New York: William Morrow, 1995.

Young, Alan. *The Pilgrim Jubilees* Jackson: University Press of Mississippi, 2001.

———. *Woke Me Up This Morning: Black Gospel Singers and the Gospel Life.* Jackson: University Press of Mississippi, 1997.

Zolten, Jerry. *Great God A'Mighty! The Dixie Hummingbirds: Celebrating the Rise of Soul Gospel Music.* New York: Oxford University Press, 2003.

ABOUT PARACLETE PRESS

Who We Are

As the publishing arm of the Community of Jesus, Paraclete Press presents a full expression of Christian belief and practice—from Catholic to Evangelical, from Protestant to Orthodox, reflecting the ecumenical charism of the Community and its dedication to sacred music, the fine arts, and the written word. We publish books, recordings, sheet music, and video/DVDs that nourish the vibrant life of the church and its people.

What We Are Doing

BOOKS | PARACLETE PRESS BOOKS show the richness and depth of what it means to be Christian. While Benedictine spirituality is at the heart of who we are and all that we do, our books reflect the Christian experience across many cultures, time periods, and houses of worship.

We have many series, including *Paraclete Essentials*; *Paraclete Fiction*; *Paraclete Poetry*; *Paraclete Giants*; and for children and adults, *All God's Creatures*, books about animals and faith; and *San Damiano Books*, focusing on Franciscan spirituality. Others include *Voices from the Monastery* (men and women monastics writing about living a spiritual life today), *Active Prayer*, and new for young readers: *The Pope's Cat*. We also specialize in gift books for children on the occasions of Baptism and First Communion, as well as other important times in a child's life, and books that bring creativity and liveliness to any adult spiritual life.

The MOUNT TABOR BOOKS series focuses on the arts and literature as well as liturgical worship and spirituality; it was created in conjunction with the Mount Tabor Ecumenical Centre for Art and Spirituality in Barga, Italy.

MUSIC | The PARACLETE RECORDINGS label represents the internationally acclaimed choir *Gloriæ Dei Cantores*, the *Gloriæ Dei Cantores Schola*, and the other instrumental artists of the *Arts Empowering Life Foundation*.

Paraclete Press is the exclusive North American distributor for the Gregorian chant recordings from St. Peter's Abbey in Solesmes, France. Paraclete also carries all of the Solesmes chant publications for Mass and the Divine Office, as well as their academic research publications.

In addition, PARACLETE PRESS SHEET MUSIC publishes the work of today's finest composers of sacred choral music, annually reviewing over 1,000 works and releasing between 40 and 60 works for both choir and organ.

VIDEO | Our video/DVDs offer spiritual help, healing, and biblical guidance for a broad range of life issues including grief and loss, marriage, forgiveness, facing death, understanding suicide, bullying, addictions, Alzheimer's, and Christian formation.

Learn more about us at our website:
www.paracletepress.com
or phone us toll-free at 1.800.451.5006

SCAN
TO
READ
MORE

YOU MAY ALSO BE INTERESTED IN THESE. . . .

READ
Billy Graham: An Ordinary Man and His Extraordinary God
Lon Allison, Foreword by Dr. Leighton Ford and Jean Graham Ford
ISBN 978-1-64060-205-2 | $14.99 | Trade paper

•

Echoes of Eternity: Listening to the Father
Hal M. Helms
ISBN 978-1-55725-173-2 | Trade paper

———

LISTEN
Appalachian Sketches
Gloriæ Dei Cantores, featuring Mark O'Connor's "Let Us Move"
ISBN 978-1-55725-281-4 | $16.99 | CD

•

Kaleidoscope: America's Faith in Song
Gloriæ Dei Cantores
ISBN 978-1-55725-542-6 | $16.99 | CD

———

SING
Steal Away to Jesus / SSAATTBB
Dale Adelmann
PPMO9512 | $1.60

•

Amazing Grace / SSAATTBB, violin, cello
Arr. Hale, Jordan, McKendree
PPMO0738 | $4.20

Available at bookstores
Paraclete Press | 1-800-451-5006
www.paracletepress.com